Hawaii
A to Z

Robert S. Kane

HAWAII
A to Z

Doubleday & Company, Inc. / Garden City, New York

Research Editor: Max Drechsler
Map of Hawaii: Rafael Palacios

Library of Congress Cataloging in Publication Data

Kane, Robert S
   Hawaii A to Z.

   (His A to Z world travel guides)
   Bibliography: p. 171
   Includes index.
   1. Hawaii—Description and travel—1951–   —Guidebooks. I. Title.
DU622.K36   919.69′04′4
ISBN 0-385-09528-7 Trade
      0-385-09525-2 Paperbound
Library of Congress Catalog Card Number 74–18813

For Kit and Patrick McCoy

Contents

Foreword

The Great American Travel Experience

Now I didn't say *typically* American. Hawaii is anything but. The idea of a full-fledged state of the union occupying the world's most isolated cluster of islands, and peopled by a non-white majority, is departure enough from the norm. Add a visitor population hovering close to three million each year, and it becomes immediately apparent that Hawaii is nothing less than a planetary phenomenon.

What is the secret of all this success? What brings us, planeload after planeload, on a two-thousand-mile flight—and often longer—from the Mainland? I suspect that it is the oddball composition of the state, a peculiarly American homogenization of a crazy, mixed bag of cultures and races and political forces, the lot having mostly interacted in the same span of two centuries that began with the American Declaration of Independence. It was just about that time that Captain Cook came upon the islands, ending something like a millennium of Isolationist Hawaii.

If we can say on the Mainland that our first two centuries were action-packed, Hawaii can maintain that in proportion to its size, that same period was for it an even more concentrated evolution. The islands' history was not without conflict—stern missionaries versus hearty whalers; those same missionaries' affluent descendants versus the oddly British-accented monarchy they themselves encouraged; mostly Oriental immigrants (sugar workers upon arrival) establishing footholds in island society against originally tough odds; later clashes between the American-descended economic Establishment that favored annexation under the Stars and Stripes, and an increasingly nationalist, Hawaii-for-Hawaiians monarchy.

Annexation was not only a bloodless political coup, it proved extraordinarily effortless in other areas, too. The late nineteenth-century Hawaiian was essentially English-speaking and had come to regard the ways of the American as not especially exotic. While the locals absorbed even more Americana, the mores of the mostly Asian newcomers—Japanese, Chinese, Filipinos, Koreans—made their impact. The geographical crossroads of the Pacific had become that same region's cultural crossroads, too.

The point is that no group, over all of those long generations, appeared to have disliked Hawaii. Quite the contrary. Virtually everybody who went stayed on. (Indeed, white Mainlanders are doing just that, contemporarily, to the point where their increasing numbers promise to tip the racial balance, and possibly provide Hawaii, for the first time, with an ethnic majority.)

The earliest modern tourists—the pre-World War II richies who sailed to the Aloha Tower only to taxi out to the then near-bucolic Royal Hawaiian and stay the winter—were small in numbers. But they were opinion moulders enough to create an image of Hawaii as a desirable holiday destination. Rather than destroy that concept, World War II—when scores of thousands of military like me came to know and love the place—set the stage for the mass tourism that was to follow. The jet aircraft was just the post-war shot in the arm that was needed.

As for the rest, Hawaii has become the Great American Travel Experience. It is, by and large, just what we want when we go on vacation. Cleanliness is next to godliness. Good looks dominate over the garish. Even Waikiki, though overbuilt, is not one whit honky-tonk. Each time I have returned over the years—and these visits were at regular intervals—I have half-feared a tacky maze of neon and worse. But I need not have worried; neither Waikiki nor the Neighbor Islands have succumbed to vulgarity.

What has happened is that the tourist plant has been developed to accommodate the budget, middling and luxury traveler with plenty of places to stay (some environmentalists and conservationists say too many). Although the cuisine, interestingly, is accented with dishes contributed by the islands' various ethnic groups, it is dominantly Mainland style. So are the diversions—the kind of beaches, golf courses and tennis courts we like, and after-dark action that is most assuredly Hawaiian in theme, but American in organization. In the pages following, after a first chapter on what has gone before, I delineate the Tourist's Hawaii, breaking it down much as I have other areas of the world in the other volumes of the A to Z series, with personally experienced places to visit, stay in, eat and drink at, as well as chapters on day and evening activity, shopping—based on intensive scouting expeditions on the major islands—and a final section of specifics ranging from climate to clothes, tours to telephone numbers.

Most American of all, to me, is the democratic aspect of tourism in Hawaii. (I think this is why foreign visitors—many Japanese but nationals of other countries, too—for whom Hawaii is often a first exposure to the United States, are so taken with it.) It is in State No. 50, as perhaps nowhere else in America, that we see ourselves at play, relaxed and looking our smiling best—rich and not so rich, white or yellow or brown or black, all Americans. Resident or visitor, we swim from the same beaches, drink at the same bars, watch the same shows, fill the same hotels, golf on the same links, crowd the same tour buses. We don't always realize it until we return home, but the perspective on our country and fellow-citizens gained from the vantage point of these detached mid-Pacific islands, ranks right up there with sun, sand and surf as a major attribute of a Hawaiian holiday. If Hawaii is not the paradise of the travel brochures—given its complexities it could hardly be without problems—it is at least as far as we have gone in that direction: an unlikely manifestation of the American dream. And an uncommonly agreeable one.

Robert S. Kane

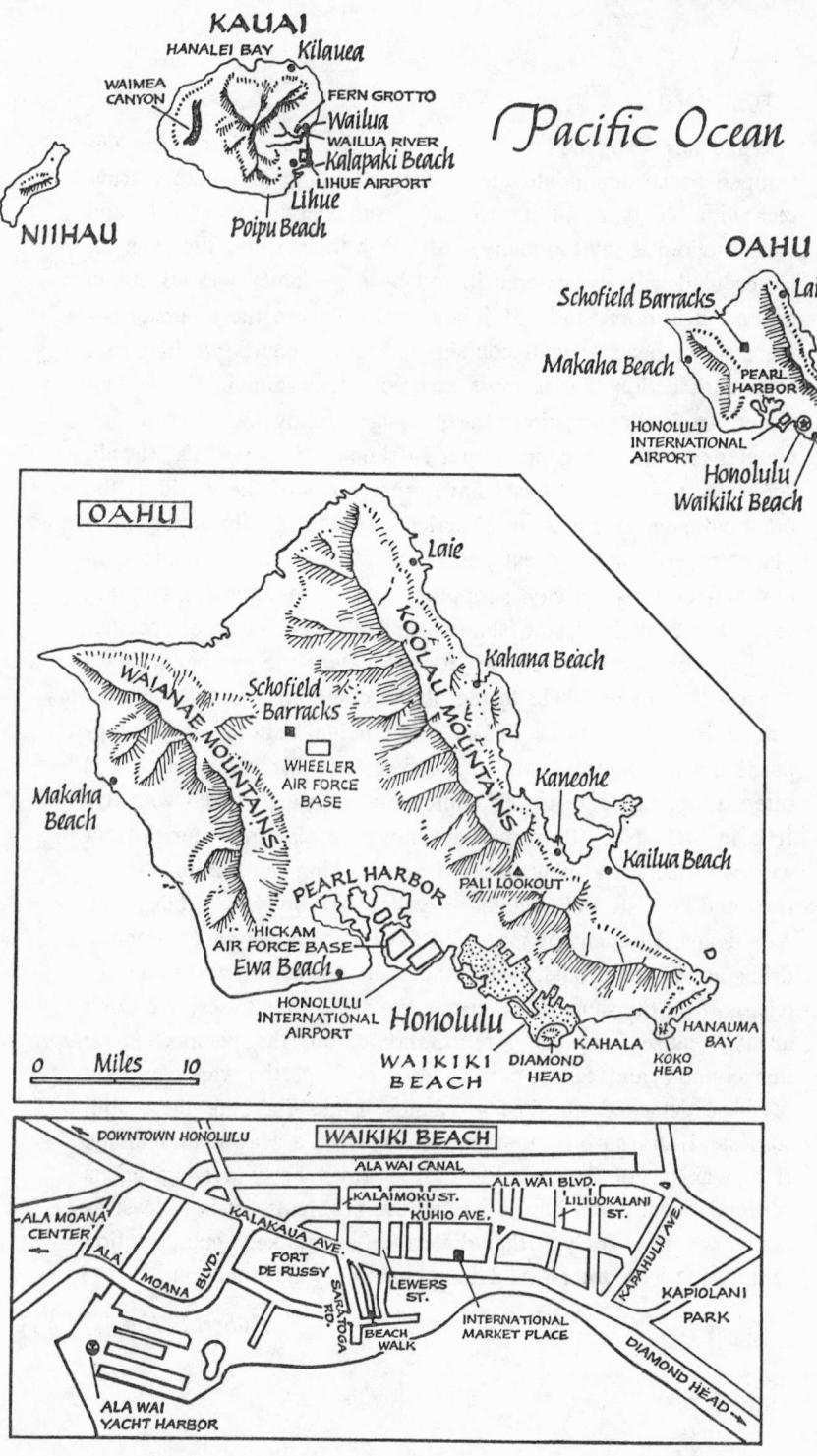

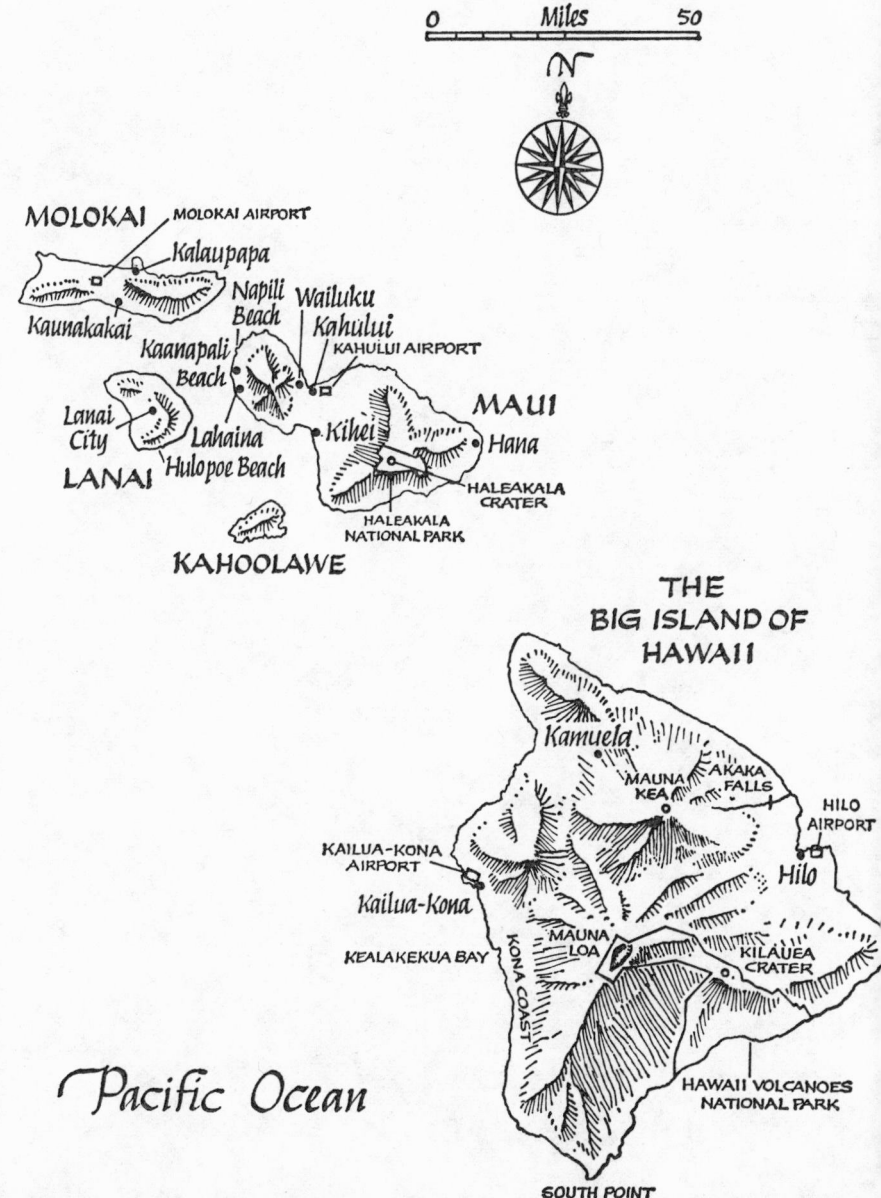

Hawaii A to Z

0   Miles   50

N

MOLOKAI
MOLOKAI AIRPORT
Kalaupapa
Kaunakakai
Napili Beach
Wailuku
Kahului
KAHULUI AIRPORT
Kaanapali Beach
Lanai City
Lahaina
Hulopoe Beach
LANAI
Kihei
MAUI
Hana
HALEAKALA CRATER
HALEAKALA NATIONAL PARK
KAHOOLAWE

THE BIG ISLAND OF HAWAII
Kamuela
MAUNA KEA
AKAKA FALLS
HILO AIRPORT
KAILUA-KONA AIRPORT
Kailua-Kona
KEALAKEKUA BAY
KONA COAST
MAUNA LOA
Hilo
KILAUEA CRATER
HAWAII VOLCANOES NATIONAL PARK
SOUTH POINT

Pacific Ocean

Hawaii
A to Z

1

Hawaii to Know

Air travel is miraculously rapid, so much so that it can rob us of the kind of perspective we got in the dim dark past—all of a quarter-century or so ago—when we mostly traveled everywhere abroad by ship. My first trip to Hawaii was out of Treasure Island in San Francisco, on a raw, gloomy, fog-swept day during World War II. Sniffly cold and sore throat or no, the Navy was sending me Pacificwards. I always remember it because it was my first and roughest-ever sea voyage. (The Pacific between California and Hawaii is by no means always pacific.) Virtually all of my fellow enlisted men were sick over the lower decks, and the greater part of the officers gaining the fresh air from the decks over our heads, were similarly afflicted. I distinctly recall our having to look up, upon reaching the railings for relief, before facing out to sea; Naval officers had precedence over sailors in all matters, even including *mal de mer*.

Five long-suffering days later, we anchored in the immense natural port that is Pearl Harbor. My cold symptoms had completely disappeared and my voice had returned (I always credit Hawaii for the cure). It was clear and bright and sunny and so ravishingly tropic-beautiful that I momentarily forgot the war and even momentarily loved the Navy for transporting me to such a place; a first encounter with a mid-Pacific island to a nine-

teen-year-old out of Albany, New York, is, to understate, a posi-
tive experience. I wondered if Captain Cook and his crew were
as excited, with their first view of Hawaii in the eighteenth century, as I was in the twentieth. And I thought how devilishly
clever was the Navy, of which I was then a member, to have
successfully persuaded Uncle Sam to negotiate rights—something
like a century and a half after Cook's arrival—for the then so-
called Pearl River Lagoon.

The point I make is that time spent at sea, even as a sad-sack
sailor, can't help but give one enough pause to assess the fortunes
of earlier travelers on the same route. In the case of Hawaii,
there were Polynesian mariners of extraordinary skill, courage
and—quite obviously—curiosity, who piloted their sleek albeit
simple craft through thousands of miles of open sea before
reaching the isolated islands that were to become their home.

THE EARLY HAWAIIANS: PADDLERS FROM WAY SOUTH

What appears to have happened is that some thirteen hundred
years ago, people from the Marquesas Islands in the South Pacific made the first paddle-power migrations to the north. They
were followed a few centuries later by Tahitians, whose archipelago is even farther south than the Marquesas. Both groups
are believed to have had considerable knowledge of astronomy,
so that the stars helped them navigate. The homeland they chose
—our State No. 50—is nothing less than the most isolated
cluster of islands, not only in the Pacific but on the planet. The
culture they brought north with them—and that included the
language—was distinctly Polynesian. It remains similar enough
—even today with all the refinements and foreign exposure it
has been confronted with—to be compared with that of fellow-
Polynesian societies in Tahiti, the Samoas and that of the Maoris
in New Zealand.

The culture was based on a rigid authoritarian society, of
which perhaps the most peculiar aspect was a system of male
dominance so all-encompassing that it even ran to matters culi-
nary. Women were so discriminated against that they could not

eat many of the same foods that their husbands did, nor—perish forbid!—could they eat in the company of the men. The system was based upon a series of *kapus,* or forbidden things. (It is interesting to note that the word *kapu* in Hawaiian is the counterpart of the better-known Tahitian word, *tabu.* Comparison of the two indicates the similarities of these two people's languages.) Hawaiian society was essentially a simple one based upon agriculture and fishing, with each of the islands more or less under control of its own chief, and the chiefs or nobles—*alii* in Hawaiian—at the top of an anything-but-democratic social system.

THE FIRST EUROPEANS

There was no written language, but as in so many highly developed spoken-culture societies, one generation learned from its predecessors through the spoken word; in the case of Hawaii, song and dance highlighted the cultural framework. Over the centuries, there was relatively little change in the pattern, so that by the time the first Westerners came upon the islands, their society—not unsurprisingly, considering its physical isolation from the rest of the world—was quite as it had been for a very long while. Even in 1825—by which time there had been contact with Europeans for nearly half a century, a Scottish botanist, James Macrae—who accompanied the bodies of King Kamehameha II and his queen back from London, where the two had died—found the people living quite traditionally, with taro patches surrounding their ancient-design grass houses, and a diet composed principally of the poi that came from the taro, and the fish that came from the sea.

"Lahaina," Macrae wrote in his journal (Petroglyph Press, Hilo), "has no regular streets, being all cultivated and rather difficult to get from one end to the other on account of the taro ponds. It looked like a well cultivated garden divided into allotments by mud walls enclosing each family hut and garden. Sugar canes grow with little trouble . . ."

By the time Macrae arrived, united Hawaii was into the reign of its third monarch—an evolution in its history not easily come by. Indeed, the chief, who through his skills as politician, persuader and warrior was able to bring the major islands together under his control, as Kamehameha I, is the only one of the monarchy's eight sovereigns dubbed "The Great." Kamehameha the Great started the process of consolidation on his home island, Hawaii, about 1790, later conquering Maui and then Oahu, with Kauai—most westerly and detached of the group—the last to be subdued.

UNIFIER OF THE ISLANDS: KAMEHAMEHA THE GREAT

Kamehameha the Great, it developed, was to be the only ruler of the monarchial octet whose reign was culturally undiluted Hawaiian. The *kapu* system, which he and his fellow *alii* inherited from their ancestors, was his law of the land. The Hawaiian gods were worshipped, the Hawaiian foods eaten, the Hawaiian economy was essentially the traditional one, supplemented by a period of trade with China in sandalwood. Captain James Cook had come upon the islands in 1778, naming them after the Earl of Sandwich, who was then First Lord of the British Admiralty. Cook met his death a year later—at the hands of Hawaiians at Kealakekua on the Big Island.

Other mariners from the West followed Cook. But their influence was minimal. Only a year after Kamehameha I died, the first party of Protestant missionaries arrived from New England. This small group and their successors—a few hundred persons in all—went to Hawaii to gain converts. They were fundamentalist Congregationalists, so strict in interpreting their faith that Christmas was considered a frivolous holiday and was not observed in Hawaii until decades after their arrival.

MISSIONARIES AND WHALERS

As history would have it, the missionaries arrived on the scene concurrently with the crews of the whalers. One need pick up any of many accounts of life at the time, especially in ports like Lahaina—which became the whaling capital of the world—to appreciate the antagonisms of these disparate groups: missionaries and their families, on the one hand, and the sailors of the ships, on the other, with the Hawaiians frequently caught in between.

Today's Hawaiians are fond of telling visitors that when the missionaries came, they had all the Bibles and the Hawaiians all the land, but that today, the Hawaiians all have Bibles, and the missionaries—or at least their prosperous descendants—have all the land. What happened, of course, is that the Hawaiians devoured the missionaries' pedagogy. There is probably no people on earth without a written language of its own that became fully literate with such incredible rapidity. As their pupils began to take their place in what was becoming a Western-economy society, certain men of the cloth began to appreciate that money was to be made in the Sandwich Islands. And political power to be achieved. The temptation was too great for some. They resigned their posts as clergymen and turned to matters mercantile. Their descendants became the nucleus of the economic Big Five of Hawaii.

And as a consequence, nineteenth-century Hawaii, from the time of Kamehameha II through to Liliuokalani, the last reigning monarch, was one long series of clashes—some much less quiet and well-mannered than others—between the increasingly affluent descendants of Americans and the royal descendants of Polynesians. The *haole*—white—Establishment wanted things their way, which meant essentially a puppet monarchy based on the British system but with economic policies favoring both local whites and Mainland America. The monarchy, one king after the other, found itself in an almost untenable cultural crosscurrent. These recent descendants of Pacific islanders had been propped up with the superficial trappings of rulers of an empire—Britain's—that had its seat on a distinctly northern island half a world away.

MONARCHY, BRITISH STYLE

A consequence was that the Hawaiian kings and queens often gave the impression of emulating their European counterparts, more as regards style than substance. Kamehameha II inherited the throne his no-nonsense papa established. To his credit, he lost no time in acceding to the requests of powerful females of his late father's court, that he disband the ancient *kapu* system. But, poor man, in other areas he tried too hard. So anxious were he and his wife to learn the ways of modern monarchy that they crossed half the globe to see how things were being done in the opulent court of King George IV. One after the other, they died tragically of measles, not long after their arrival in London.

Kamehameha III followed his brother to the throne, and had a substantial three-decade reign—the longest of the monarchy. The evolution toward ways Western, begun by his brother, became refined to the point where Hawaii achieved not only its first constitution, but its first legislature. Concurrently, there were other manifestations of progress: a secondary school—the first west of the Rockies—opened on Maui; the Pacific area's first newspaper appeared, sugar was cultivated as a cash crop, and the capital moved from lusty Lahaina to quieter, less-celebrated Honolulu, on Oahu. That happened in 1845, only two years after a happily brief bit of madness which saw the Kingdom of Hawaii lose its sovereignty to Britain, the result of one Lord George Paulet's maneuverings, following a diplomatic tiff between the two countries. The oddball British usurpation lasted but a few months. By the time Kamehameha III and his court moved to Honolulu, the Polynesian kingdom's independence had been recognized by the Pacific's Big Three—Britain, France and the United States.

SUGAR—AND A WAVE OF IMMIGRATION

Kamehameha III's reign saw the start of a remarkable series of immigrations occasioned by the commencement of a sugar industry that needed laborers. The Chinese were the first (1852), and the Lyman House Museum in Hilo succinctly lists the others in one of its exhibits, as follows: Portuguese (1878), Japanese (1885), Koreans (1903), Filipinos (1906). These, the museum points out, were supplemented by smaller inputs from other places: South Sea islanders (1859), Scots (1880s), Scandinavians (1881), Germans (1881), Galician Poles (1897), Puerto Ricans (1900), Spaniards (1907) and Russians (1909). The immigrants had adjustments to make. "They had"—again to quote the same museum's exhibit legend—"to adjust to plantation life, alien languages, a new physical environment, new types of food, clothing, housing and transportation, a new form of government and a new type of education."

This was, of course, an evolutionary process. While the immigrants were adjusting, the industry that drew so many of them—sugar—developed not only in acreage but as a force in the islands' political life. The sugar interests began to tire of the monarchy, even though it was heavily guided by ex-missionaries and other *haoles* who held the preponderance of cabinet posts. (If any one missionary-politician stands out as the dominant non-Hawaiian political figure of the nineteenth century, it is Dr. Gerrit P. Judd, trained as both physician and clergyman. He was the power behind the throne of Kamehameha III, whose thirty-year reign was the longest of any monarch, and he remained a political force well into the end of the reign of the succeeding Kamehameha.) By the time Kamehameha IV ascended the throne in 1854, a movement was afoot—it was to last half a century—advocating annexation by Uncle Sam. It was opposed by one monarch after the other, each in his or her own way. Kamehameha IV acted against not only the annexationists, but the New England missionary descendants, by establishing the Church of England (now the Episcopal Church) in Hawaii. Indeed, his part-*haole* wife, Queen Emma, went to England to raise money—and to find an architect—for the construction of Honolulu's St. Andrew's Cathedral. (Her royal relatives, during the period she was Dowager Queen Emma, never quite forgave her her Anglican leanings; they, of course, were all associated with the missionary-founded Kawaiahao Church.)

KINGS VS. ANNEXATIONISTS

Emma's husband reigned for about a decade, dying a premature twenty-nine. His successor, a brother—the fifth and last

Kamehameha—ruled for still another decade (1863–72). These two, as young princes, had raised eyebrows when they had traveled through Europe under the chaperonage of the aforementioned Dr. Judd. Like his predecessor, Kamehameha V was not only pro-Anglican Church but anti-missionary, enough so to foster the reintroduction of aspects of the traditional Hawaiian culture done away with by the stern missionaries. And where would today's Hawaii—and its tourists—have been without him: The hula dance was the chief of these.

It was during his reign that the annexationists and the monarchists focused their antagonism toward each other over the issue of a new constitution. The king wanted a less democratic one, fearing that a liberal document would make easier a transition to a republic—and ultimate U.S. annexation. The sugar interests fought on the other side, and lost. Hawaii's second constitution (1864) was just what the royals wanted: its pro-monarchy bias had the desired effect of seeing the crown through another near-quarter century.

It might be as well at this point—with the death of the last Kamehameha—to simplify the terminology with respect to the first five kings, all of whom were *officially* named Kamehameha. But, to confuse matters, especially among those of us to whom Hawaiian history is much more remote than, say, English history, Numbers II, III, IV and V all had second, personal names of their own, by which they are sometimes called. Kamehameha II was also known as Liholiho. Kamehameha III was Kauikeaouli to his intimates. Kamehameha IV was Alexander Liholiho. Kamehameha V was Lot.

TOWARD THE END OF MONARCHY

With Lot's death, that part of the family that had produced the quintet of Kamehamehas became extinct, so that it became necessary to elect a successor from among a quintet of candidates. Princess Bernice Pauahi Bishop, the very same who married banker Charles Bishop, who founded the Bishop Museum in her memory, declined the honor; Kamehameha V had nominated her to be his successor just before he died. That left the rotund, non-English-speaking Princess Ruth; Dowager Queen Emma, widow of Kamehameha IV; Prince David Kalakaua (who was later to have his turn); and Prince William Charles Lunalilo, who had some blood-connections with Kamehameha I, and who was the victor. Sadly, he died within a year, opening up Hawaii to still another monarchial election.

This time, both Dowager Queen Emma and Prince David Kalakaua, losers in the election only a year earlier, entered the fray again, and it is quite possible that no monarchy has ever witnessed a rowdier royal election. When Queen Emma's followers learned that David Kalakaua was declared winner they rioted; the government had to call in foreigners—American troops and British marines both—to calm things down.

The new ruler—and last king—chose the name Kalakaua; history knows him also as the Merry Monarch. Not unlike his predecessors he was bitten by the travel bug. But Britain was not destination enough. Kalakaua opted for the world and has gone down on the record as the first reigning monarch—of any country anywhere—to circumnavigate the globe. When he got home, he had with him a pair of crowns picked up in England for his consort, Queen Kapiolani, and himself. He had the Iolani Palace we know today built as an official residence, along with the bandstand on the grounds, which he ordered—and used—as his coronation stand.

A QUEEN DEPOSED—AND THE REPUBLIC

Not quite so merry was the new constitution he was obliged to sign—limiting the sovereign's power, and making the monarchy a constitutional one, with the cabinet responsible to the legislature rather than to the sovereign. During his reign, Kalakaua sent his well-educated sister, Crown Princess Liliuokalani, with non-English-speaking Queen Kapiolani to Queen Victoria's diamond jubilee celebrations in London. All the while, his troubles with the

Establishment whites—by then mostly banded together as the Missionary, or Reform Party—were increasing.

He decided, rather suddenly, in 1891, to take a break, and set sail for San Francisco where, 'ere long, he died in the Palace—now the Sheraton Palace—Hotel. His sister, the wife of Englishman John Dominis, moved across Beretania Street from Washington Place—the lovely white frame house built by her husband's parents that is now the Executive Mansion—into Iolani Palace. She reigned for almost two years as Queen Liliuokalani. If you have a chance, pick up her autobiography, *Hawaii's Story by Hawaii's Queen*. You admire this articulate, keenly intelligent, strong-willed lady, whether or not you agree with all of her decidedly royalist views. Liliuokalani fought the annexationists bravely but in vain. She lost, but like a lady, in a bloodless revolution that saw her deposed and, for a period of nine months, imprisoned in an upstairs Iolani Palace bedroom. Upon her release, she was allowed to leave the country for a Mainland visit, during which time she met with President McKinley, whose administration—unlike that of the earlier President Cleveland's—agreed to annexation. Liliuokalani's successor was Sanford Ballard Dole, a New England cousin of whose was later to have his name become synonymous with Hawaiian pineapple. Dole headed a Provisional Government whose request for annexation was refused by Cleveland, after which—in 1894—it converted itself into the Republic of Hawaii, with Dole as President. (To the deposed Liliuokalani, this was the "so-called" Republic of Hawaii.) In 1898, the Democratic Cleveland's Republican successor, McKinley, went along with annexation; it was the period of the Spanish American War and the Islands' strategic position became attractive to Washington.

1898: HAWAII, U.S.A.

A joint resolution of Congress made it official: Hawaii was annexed August 12, 1898, and when it became the Territory of Hawaii—which it was to remain well over half a century—its first governor was the very same Sanford B. Dole.

The irony of Hawaii's political evolution is that everybody has come out a winner. The descendants of the missionaries—those stubborn, quite literally Puritanical early nineteenth-century proselytizers who, almost despite themselves, brought Hawaii into contact with the West and gave its people Instant Literacy—became rich. The Hawaiians were set on the road to political strength and increasing economic prowess. And the Islands' Mainland neighbors gained a remarkable group of fellow-citizens occupying a remarkable cluster of islands.

1941: PEARL HARBOR

But full-citizenship was a long time coming. Territorial Hawaii built slowly. Tourism had its beginnings in the twenties when the Royal Hawaiian Hotel went up to complement the nearby Moana which had been the only hotel of substance since it was built in 1901. The thirties saw the build-up of the long-neglected naval base at Pearl Harbor. When the Japanese Air Force attacked at 7:55 A.M. on December 7, 1941, just about the entire Pacific fleet was neatly tucked into the capacious harbor's berths. Several thousand casualties ensued. President Roosevelt, in his classic "Day of Infamy" speech, announced that the United States was at war. Hawaii—or so it seemed to at least one visitor who remembers it from that period—was one great military base.

The post-war years saw accelerated political development. Labor strengthened itself considerably in the sugar and pineapple plantations and on the waterfront, and concurrently, popular sentiment for statehood became a dominant fact of Hawaiian life. (The first statehood bill had been proposed after World War I by the respected—and voteless—Territorial Delegate to Congress, Prince Jonah Kuhio Kalanianaole.) Post-World War II lobbying for statehood was a major accomplishment of Delegate Joseph Farrington and later, his widow and successor, Elizabeth. While John A. Burns—later to become state governor—was Delegate in 1959, Congress enacted the Statehood bill, and President Eisenhower signed it into law. Hawaii became State No. 50—the first island state and the first state without a racial majority—on August 21, 1959. (Although the first two state governors—William F. Quinn and Mr. Burns—were white, voters in 1974 gave America its first governor—Democrat, George R. Ariyoshi—of Japanese descent. Earlier, Hawaii had sent citizens of both Chinese [Hiram L. Fong] and Japanese [Daniel K. Inouye] descent to the U. S. Senate, pioneering also with its two-member delegation to the Lower House, with Mrs. Patsy Takemoto Mink and Spark M. Matsunaga, both of Japanese origin. Still, despite the ascendancy of Oriental-origin citizens in the state's political leadership, white migration from the Mainland had become substantial enough, by the mid-seventies as to make possible a Caucasian majority. If such occurs, it will be the first racial majority—of any kind—in the state's history.)

STATEHOOD AND MASS TOURISM

By that time, the post-World War II tourism phenomenon was well underway, while sugar and pineapple continued as the major sources of income. Although sugar remains important, pineapple may be phased out as an export crop, and it is as well that the visitor industry—Hawaii's euphemism for tourism—is there to take its place in the economy. Still, even tourism creates problems. With the yearly visitor total nearing the neighborhood of three million—in a state whose area makes it No. 47 of the 50 and whose population is under a million—tourism's effects on the environment are making themselves felt. No one argues the value of the revenue brought in—close to a billion dollars annually. Still, only toward the end of the decade of the sixties, and as the seventies began, did the people of Hawaii begin to realize that overbuilding the visitor plant could be self-defeating. While no one was looking, several high-rises went up at the foot of Waikiki Beach's Diamond Head, ruining its lovely profile forever—or at least for as long as they stand. Whereas the beach had only a trio of ocean-front hotels for many years, it now has several times that number, sadly squeezed alongside each other.

Better late than never, fears began to be expressed publicly as to the consequences of uncontrolled building in rural Oahu, and of heavy high-rise building on the beautiful Neighbor Islands. Politicians now debate the pros and cons of controlled growth. Environment and conservation are now commonplace terms on everyone's lips, pro or con. Even the hardliners are beginning to appreciate that skyscraping Waikiki Beach is the only highly developed resort area the state needs. And that Neighbor Island or rural-Oahu counterparts of Waikiki might well be straws breaking the touristic camel's back. What visitors cross two thousand miles of Pacific Ocean for, more than anything else, is natural beauty. Replace that with sky-is-the-limit hotels, and we might just as well stay at home.

2

Hawaii to See

LAY OF THE LAND

It is understandable, if not forgivable, if a visitor from abroad, or even an American, were to confuse, say, North with South Dakota, parts of Arizona with neighboring New Mexico, New Hampshire with Vermont, Illinois with Indiana, Alabama with Georgia. But Hawaii is one-of-a-kind: it is, of course, America's only island state. Some 2,000 miles from the California coast, it is still another 2,000 miles from its nearest neighbors among the Pacific island clusters. There is not, as a matter of fact, another island group on the planet that is more isolated.

Nor is there excessive room to roam. If you get right down to it, our youngest state is almost our smallest—No. 47 in area, just after New Jersey, with only Connecticut, Delaware and Rhode Island more minuscule. And even with its constantly increasing population—permanent, that is, not tourist—Hawaii is No. 40 of the states, with something like a million full-time inhabitants.

At this point, let me point out that because of its peculiar ethnic composition, Hawaii's residents cannot all accurately be called Hawaiian. Any resident of Iowa can call himself an Iowan, but you are a Hawaiian only if you are descended—fully or at least in part—from the Islands' original Polynesian inhabitants. Otherwise, Hawaii categorizes its residents as Caucasian or *haole* ("white" is used considerably less frequently than on the Mainland, which is what the other forty-nine United States are collectively called). Then there are the Oriental groups—Japanese, Chinese, Filipino, Korean, as well as a small black minority, and non-Hawaiian Polynesian segments of the populace, with Samoans constituting the bulk of this last-named group. There are, additionally, infinite racial mixtures. Hawaii is about as melting pot as an American state can get, and unique in that no ethnic group as yet constitutes a majority.

Geographically, this volcanic-origin chain—some 1,500 miles in total length—is not difficult to size up. Although there are 124 islands in the state's 6,450 square miles, as well as another half dozen or so without its bounds, only eight of these are of any consequence. One of that group—Kahoolawe—may be immediately discounted as it is uninhabited. Another—Niihau—might just as well be, as far as the outer world is concerned. Privately owned and operated, it is home to but a few hundred pure-blooded Hawaiians—agricultural workers, who still live in the traditional style of their ancestors and toil for a branch of one of the old Caucasian families, which allows absolutely no visitors (and that includes the press) other than invited guests. (What other American state is possessed of such an anachronism?)

Discount two more of the remaining half-dozen islands—Molokai, which is just beginning to concern itself with tourism, and even less visitor-prepared Lanai—and the vacationer's Hawaii embraces but a quartet of islands: Oahu, Hawaii, Maui, and Kauai.

It is Oahu that looms largest of the Big Four, although not because of its physical proportions—it is No. 3 in square miles and No. 4 as regards the height of its peaks. Oahu's ace in the hole is Honolulu, the capital, whose principal resort sector—Waikiki Beach—has become a planetary synonym for vacation locale. Oahu, thanks to these assets, is home to some seven of every ten of the state's residents, not to mention the overwhelming majority of vacationers. When you name "Hawaii" as your holiday destination, you are, by and large, talking about Oahu. Even then, you may narrow that down to the Waikiki sector.

The larger city—Honolulu—remains, rather incredibly, a touristic *terra incognita,* and so does much of the remainder of the island. Which is not to say that this is the ideal situation. One of the aims of this book will be to divert the reader from Waikiki to the core of the capital, as well as to rural Oahu.

Hawaii, the largest-in-area island of the group, from which the archipelago takes its collective name, is known, more often than not, as the Big Island. Embracing more than four thousand square miles, it is about twice as large as the other three top islands' combined areas. Which makes the Big Island's population—close to 70,000—spare in proportion to its size, even though it is second to Oahu's. On the Big Island one may ski from the slopes of one of the world's highest volcanic peaks. Or swim on the same day, although this island's natural beaches are in surprisingly short supply. There are, for example, none to speak of on the historic Kona coast, or in the region of Hilo, the principal town and the only proper city in the state, after Honolulu. Pool-swimming is the rule on Hawaii, the major exception being the magnificent strand at the hotel named for the volcanic peak of Mauna Kea.

Maui follows the Big Island in both size and population. It is as important historically as Hawaii, with venerable (by Hawaiian standards at least) Lahaina, its most visited town. Its hotel-dotted Kaanapali Beach area, adjacent to Lahaina, is its principal visitor sector. But Hana, on eastern Maui, might well be considered by the visitor seeking quiet, secluded kind of beauty. Nor are Maui's twin administrative centers—Kahului and Wailuku —to be neglected. (They're easy to visit because the island's principal airport is in the neighborhood.) And if I had to make a choice of the state's vast and splendid natural phenomena, it would be the vast and splendid dormant crater that constitutes Maui's Haleakala National Park.

Kauai is the least visited, least known, and newest-to-develop among the four major islands. It was the last of the group to become a part of King Kamehameha the Great's united chain. It is also the wettest, and as a happy consequence—at least to this visitor—the most beautiful. It follows Oahu as the fourth largest in area, and Maui, as the fourth largest in population. The principal town is little Lihue. The principal natural phenomenon is the dazzling Waimea Canyon, and there are perfectly lovely beaches.

Your Hawaiian Itinerary? It can, of course, be of your own making, or you may, like many visitors, find yourself following the path of a group itinerary. What I suggest is a taste of all four principal islands on a first Hawaiian journey. Headquarter on Oahu, but work in the Big Island, Maui and Kauai, as well. Then, when you return for subsequent Hawaiian holidays—and mind, this is an area chock-a-block full of returnees—you'll have an idea of what you want to concentrate on. You may, if you are really well organized, plan your entire island-by-island program before leaving home. But even if you arrive intending only to spend a few days at Waikiki, you may make Neighbor Islands arrangements on the spot (see Chapter 8).

THE ISLAND OF OAHU

Mention the Koolau or the Waianae mountains to your average Oahu vacationer and you get a blank look in return. The natural composition of this principal island is not something most visitors concern themselves with, if one excepts the sands of Waikiki Beach or the turf of nearby golf links. My point is that there is a good bit more to forty-mile-long Oahu than Waikiki and the Honolulu of which it is a part. Even in that regard, it is more often than not a case of the tail wagging the dog. Leave the beach for downtown of an afternoon, and you have the eerie feeling that you're the only tourist about. You get the same feeling in much of rural Oahu. Indeed, the Waikiki-bound talk themselves into the notion that their headquarters-island is devoid of natural beauty, and reserve bucolic jaunts for the Neighbor Islands. If they would look around a bit, they would realize how wrong they are: two striking mountain ranges, a verdant interior still full of cane fields and pineapple plantations, and a splendid coast—from

Diamond Head in the south to Kawela Bay way up north—most all of which is bordered by roads, and easily inspected.

As for mountains, it is the Koolau Range, running north-south, that separates Oahu into windward and leeward areas, with the high cliff known as the *Nuuanu Pali* serving both as the dividing line and as the site of one of the great vistas of the entire state.

The whole thrust of tourism, in recent seasons, has been one of decentralization. Just as the Puerto Ricans would like us to spread out from the Condado and Isla Verde sections of San Juan into the little-visited sectors of the island, so would the Hawaii Visitors Bureau and the accommodations and transport interests like us to fan out from Waikiki. But meanwhile, let's start at the beginning.

Explaining directions in Hawaiian: It may seem an affectation, and it would be easier if everyone simply said east, west, north and south. But when in Rome . . . Hawaii residents retain the old Hawaiian ways of locating places. *Makai* is toward the ocean. *Mauka* is toward the mountain (inland). On Oahu, please note that something or someplace to the east is designated as being *Waikiki, Diamond Head,* or *Koko Head* (a point east of Diamond Head) of where one is standing, depending upon one's position at the time of asking directions. For example, if you are at the Hilton Hawaiian Village Hotel and ask the doorman for the direction of the Sheraton-Waikiki Hotel, he will no doubt tell you it is Diamond Head. If you are at Pearl Harbor and ask the location of the University of Hawaii, you will be told it is Waikiki of where you are. The other direction—to the west—is, on Oahu, referred to as *ewa,* the name of a plantation area on western Oahu. For example, if you are at the International Market Place, are interested in getting to the Ala Moana Shopping Center, and ask which way it is located, you will be told it is *ewa* of the market place. If you're at the Moana Hotel and seek the King's Alley shopping center, you'll be told it's almost due *mauka.* Conversely, if you are at King's Alley, and are looking for the Moana Hotel, you'll be told it's almost due *makai.*

Waikiki Beach, not unlike other fashionable resorts in other parts of the world, was helped along by royalty—the earlier *alii,* or nobles, and in later decades, the monarchs themselves, who built "summer homes" after the fashion of European counterparts in temperate-zone countries where seasonal residences made more sense than is the case in tropical Hawaii. Queen Liliuokalani, the very grand, very regal, very European-oriented final monarch, maintained what she called a "pretty seaside cottage" at Waikiki, not far from what is currently the Hawaiian Regent Hotel. In 1869, while still a princess—and before she succeeded her brother, King Kalakaua, on the throne—she gave a *luau* for the then Duke of Edinburgh, a son of Queen Victoria. When he entered, Liliuokalani wrote in her autobiography, "he was met by two very pretty Hawaiian ladies who advanced, and according to the custom of our country, decorated him with *leis,* the long pliable wreaths of flowers suspended from the neck. He seemed a bit confused at the novel custom, but submitting with the easy grace of a gentleman, he appeared to be excessively pleased with the flowers and with the expression of friendly welcome conveyed to him by the act."

Waikiki, in Liliuokalani's time, was countryside bucolic, rich folks' territory, a good carriage ride from town. Wealthy *haole* families—mostly descended of the earlier American missionaries —followed royalty into the neighborhood. And with the turn of the century came the Moana, a proper hotel, which—miracle of miracles, and praise be to such recent landlords as Matson Line and Sheraton Hotels—still stands, still in business as a hotel, and— if one forgets a post-World War II addition—recognizable.

The post-World War I era saw the beginnings of a Waikiki tourist industry, small by contemporary standards but enough to warrant satellite guest houses in the Moana neighborhood, and the construction of the Ala Wai Canal which made possible drainage of the area's buggy swamps. The still-gracious Royal Hawaiian Hotel, built in the same modified Spanish style that was contemporarily the vogue in southern California and Florida, went up almost next door to the Moana just before the Depression of the late twenties. It was the forerunner of still other hotels put up in the following decade. By the time of Pearl Harbor, in late 1941, Waikiki had established itself as a resort of consequence. The idea was quality rather than quantity. Most visitors arrived by Matson steamer rather than by air (Matson operated both the Royal Hawaiian and the Moana before the war, and opened other hotels after the war, later bowing completely out of the picture, both as regards accommodations and transport).

World War II turned Oahu—including Waikiki—into one vast military base. That was when I first knew it. The Royal Hawaiian had been taken over by the Navy as a rehabilitation center for personnel in from combat duty farther out in the Pacific. The Moana remained open as a hotel, and Sunday dinner in its *lanai* restaurant—I recall it costing all of $1.50—was the treat of the week for countless servicemen, this then-sailor most definitely included.

The nineteen-fifties saw the airplane supplant the Matson ships, and mass tourism had its beginnings. The Moana's earlier-mentioned wing—all of eight modest stories—changed the Waikiki skyline and turned out to be the prototype, on a small scale, of what was to follow. The thirteen-story also-Matson-operated Princess Kaiulani followed, in the wake of other hostelries. Came the early sixties, and Waikiki had some 9,000 rooms, some 8,000 more than a decade before. Sheraton took over Matson's hotels, building a twenty-nine-story addition to the original Princess Kaiulani, the twenty-two-story Surfrider between the Moana and the Royal Hawaiian, and later, even an addition to the once-thought-sacrosanct Royal itself, not to mention the next-door giant Sheraton-Waikiki.

But Sheraton was only a part of the rapidly expanding hotel scene. The pioneering Niumalu, which had become industrialist Henry Kaiser's Hawaiian Village, evolved into the Hilton Hawaiian Village, greatly enlarged over the years. The Outrigger group put up a network of its own hotels. Hilton International entered the scene with the luxurious Kahala Hilton in a quietly elegant residential area away from Waikiki. Amfac, one of the original Big Five of the Hawaii economic scene, entered the travel business with tours, Neighbor Islands hotels and the Waikiki Beachcomber Hotel, in the thick of things. Franchise operations like Holiday Inn and Travelodge put up properties. While the authorities turned their collective heads, the foot of Diamond Head was built upon, with the luxurious Colony Surf and a couple of lesser hotels rearing their silhouettes on a classic horizon that should never have been allowed to become so despoiled. Meanwhile, at the downtown or, as the locals say, *ewa* end of Waikiki, the giant Ilikai, now a Western International hotel, went up with the also-towering Ala Moana, now a part of the Americana group, following.

Concurrently, less prestigious hotels—medium-sized and small—mushroomed in the area between the beach and the Ala Wai Canal. The early seventies saw a Waikiki with some 25,000 hotel rooms, and enough restaurants, snack spots, bars, lounges, night clubs and shops to make it one of the planet's best-equipped resort areas.

Emerging into the seventies, Waikiki, or at least its developers, and Honolulu's regular residents, began to have second thoughts about what they had wrought. Waikiki became known as an example of what the Neighbor Islands must never be allowed to become. Its detractors called it Miami Beach West. There is no question but that the environmentalists and conservationists are correct in citing it as an example of excessive development. The fear remains that the other islands may be allowed to emulate Waikiki, and that controls on their development may not be stringent enough.

Still, there is awareness in Hawaii that one Waikiki is quite enough, and that if the other parts of the state emulate it, there will be no reason for tourists to transport themselves great distances to see still another high-rise resort area. Withal, Waikiki has a lot going for it. Despite the masses of visitors and of commercial establishments, it remains spotlessly clean, and miraculously devoid of garish illuminated signs. I know of no major resort area—anywhere—where hotel signs are more modest, abundant with gardens, and greenery; and with streets—from

the wide, commercial Kalakaua Avenue to quiet side thorough-
fares between Kalakaua and the canal—that remains a pleasure
to stroll upon, day or evening.

To get your Waikiki bearings, consider the area an oblong, enclosed lengthwise by the Pacific Ocean and, in the interior, the Ala
Wai Canal, with Diamond Head at its eastern (or Diamond
Head) extremity, and a north-south (or *mauka-makai*) arm of
the Ala Wai Canal constituting its western (or *ewa*) boundary,
going in the direction of downtown Honolulu. Waikiki's main
street, Kalakaua (Kala-KOW-a) Avenue, is named for the last
Hawaiian king. Going inland, or *mauka,* the principal thorough-
fares running parallel to Kalakaua Avenue are Kuhio Avenue,
and, fronting the canal, Ala Wai Boulevard. One may gain downtown via either Kalakaua Avenue or Ala Moana, which is a
mauka-makai street leading from Kalakaua near the *ewa* end
of Waikiki. Principal cross-Waikiki streets, leading *mauka* from
Kalakaua Avenue to Ala Wai Boulevard, include Kalaimoku
Street, which becomes Saratoga Road, when it extends *makai* from
Kalakaua towards the beach; Lewers Street, Kaiulani Street (easily
distinguishable as it is bordered by the higher tower of the Princess Kaiulani Hotel), and bordering Kapiolani Park on the
Diamond Head side, Kapahulu Avenue.

Downtown Honolulu is, oddly enough, about as far from the
touristic beaten path as one can stray, on southern Oahu. In recent
years, youngish, upward-mobile Honolulans have begun to move
into its modern apartment complexes—such as Harbor Square,
Queen Emma Gardens and Kukui Gardens—and downtown is
enjoying a renaissance. Still, though it is the business and economic
center of the mid-Pacific, its placidity offers a contrast to the ebul-
lience of Waikiki.

Downtown is the site of the fifteen-story, eight-million-dollar
Municipal Building on King Street, and of a number of other re-
cent structures. Its Chinatown is distinct from those of the West
Coast and New York. Hotel Street, bordering it, is just the kind of

honky-tonk, sailor-on-leave street one expects in a Pacific port, running the gamut from girlie shows to porno shops. Fort Street Mall—pedestrians only—is a handsome shopping enclave. Bishop Street is Establishment Honolulu, with the headquarters of such firms as Castle and Cooke, Bank of Hawaii, and Amfac, whose building boasts a public garden six stories skyward. The Alexander Young Building—for long a leading hotel—is another downtown landmark, as are the Dillingham, Brewer and Alexander & Baldwin buildings. Not to mention the Aloha Tower—traditional tie-up point for passenger liners—and the Monarchy Promenade, Honolulu's historic core enclosed by Beretania, Richards, Queen and South streets, whose attractions—Iolani Palace and the Mission Houses Museum are but two—are described on later pages. Suffice it at this point, for me to make a plea: have a look, a good look, downtown; it's what Honolulu—indeed, what Hawaii—is all about.

Rural Oahu is less tourist-neglected than downtown Honolulu. Although, were it not for such attractions as the Polynesian Cultural Center and Sea Life Park on the east coast, and Pearl Harbor, on the south coast, one wonders if it would see much tourist traffic. In the pages following, I make suggestions on rural Oahu specifics. But let me advise here that you take off on your own for whatever points appeal on Oahu—the Kaena Point Lighthouse north of Makaha on the windward coast, Schofield Barracks and Wahiawa deep in the interior, Sunset Beach on the north shore. Not to mention unheralded little towns throughout the island that constitute its least pretentious, friendliest destinations.

THE ESSENTIAL OAHU: EIGHT REQUISITES

Bishop Museum: One dare not go by names in Hawaii. The Bishop, for example, might sound ecclesiastical or Anglo, or both. Actually, it could not be more intrinsically Hawaiian. What hap-

pened was this: Princess Bernice Pauahi, the last descendant of
King Kamehameha the Great's dynasty, inherited not only her
royal antecedents' extensive lands, but many of their Hawaiian
treasures. When she died, they went to her wealthy *haole* husband,
Charles Reed Bishop. Mr. Bishop, using the royal collection as a
nucleus, established the Bishop Museum in 1889, in his wife's
memory. Since then, it has grown considerably, and in the process
achieved an enviable reputation as one of the Pacific Basin's
foremost museums of anthropology and natural history. The principal buildings are a trio of noteworthy Richardson Romanesque
structures, of the kind called after noted U.S. architect Henry H.
Richardson, that Mainland cities are struggling to keep from de-
struction. The dilly of the lot is Hawaii Hall, an 1899 gem whose
principal exhibition hall, with its elegant koa-wood trim, is a soar-
ing three stories in height. Occupying much of the length—and
of the height—of the hall is an enormous stuffed sperm whale that
is fifty-five feet long and weighed some twenty tons when cap-
tured. This souvenir of Hawaii's great whaling era is only a
starter. Each of the three levels of Hawaii Hall has its own theme.
The first relates to ancient Hawaii; the second—my favorite—
has to do with the 4-M European influences on the Islands—
monarchs, mariners, missionaries and merchants; and the top
level is devoted to the diverse cultures that make up contemporary
Hawaii. Pick your own most-liked exhibits—the thatched Hawaiian house and the finely worked red-and-yellow feather capes
of early royalty downstairs, Captain Cook's own map of the Islands (Hawaii—the Big Island—is spelled *Owhyee,* Maui is
Mowee, and Oahu is *Woahoo*), the original thrones of King
Kalakaua and Queen Kapiolani, monarchs' crowns, precious doc-
uments. . . . The location is inconveniently away from town, but
you might want to investigate the London double-decker bus which
the museum operates between its headquarters and the Heritage
Theatre, which it also operates, at the King's Alley shopping center in Waikiki. You may buy a combination ticket that includes
round-trip bus fare, museum admission, admission as well to the

planetarium that adjoins the museum, and a ticket for the *Falls of Clyde* (later described) and to the current show at the Heritage Theatre.

The Honolulu Academy of Arts (900 South Beretania Street) appears to be one of Honolulu's best-kept cultural secrets. Chances are you will tour its galleries in the company of yourself and the guards. Very sad, this, for the Academy has a great deal going for it. There are larger Mainland cities with easier access to the great world art markets, but with less substantial collections than that of the Honolulu Academy. The building itself is a gem. Broad, low-slung and wrapped around a great central court and four lesser courts, it is a late-twenties work, tiled-roofed in the then-modish Spanish style. A single donor, Mrs. Charles M. Cooke—of one of the Big Five families—was responsible for the museum.

Entering on Beretania Street, you do best to head for the information desk and pick up a gratis *Guide to the Galleries* leaflet. From it you'll perceive that the dozen-odd galleries to the left of the capacious central court are devoted to Oriental and Pacific art, and the dozen or so galleries to the right of the central court relate to European and American art. Amble about and you see that this is a repository where both money and taste have been put to good use; Establishment Honolulu is obviously behind the Academy. And more power to it. The European-American collections run from the ancient Mediterranean world to the Medieval era, through the Renaissance, the eighteenth and nineteenth centuries on both sides of the Atlantic, right up to a Helen Frankenthaler painting and a David Smith metal sculpture. In between there are French tapestries, Italian madonnas, Gilbert Stuart and Charles Wilson Peale portraits, painted Venetian doorframes, a room full of Kress-endowed Italian masterworks, and later works by the likes of Delacroix, Whistler, Homer, Gauguin, Van Gogh, Mary Cassatt, Pissarro, Rivera and Picasso. Cross over to the Pacific galleries, and the range is broad, from magnificent Hawaiian tapa cloths, New Guinean wood carving, and African sculpture, through to Chinese brocades, jades and ceramics, to Japanese bronzes and ceremonial masks, exquisite Korean celadon bowls, Filipino laces, Persian tiles and Indian embroideries. The newspapers will apprise you of special exhibitions held in the second-floor galleries. There's a sleeper of a restaurant, recommended in Chapter 5. Also, the Alice Cooke Spalding House, a satellite of the Academy in another part of town, is described in later pages.

Iolani Palace: It took the Hawaiian monarchy some time to get around to construction of a proper palace—the only royal digs on American soil. Only the last two of the reigning monarchs—Kalakaua, followed by his sister, Liliuokalani—actually lived in Iolani (although there was an earlier, simpler version that went up half a century earlier). The current palace is Italian Renaissance with a tropical twist, reminding me of nothing so much as the Hall of Languages, where I studied English (with some success) and Spanish (with much less) at Syracuse University. Both buildings went up at roughly the same time; Iolani was occupied by Kalakaua in 1882, with the first shindig a dinner for 120 of his fellow-Masons just after Christmas that year. After his death, his sister, who had been Crown Princess and was living across the street in Washington Place (now the Executive Mansion) moved in, remaining not only for the two years of her reign but, after she had been deposed, for nine additional months as a prisoner. Freed, she recrossed Beretania Street to Washington Place, remaining there until she died toward the end of World War I. Meanwhile, the government of the Republic of Hawaii took over Iolani as its headquarters, and it remained the center of the action for the government of the Territory of Hawaii, after annexation. With Statehood, the governor moved in, using King Kalakaua's bedroom as his office, while the Legislature met in two downstairs chambers—the Throne Room, which became the House of Representatives, with the State Dining Room seeing service as the Senate. With the opening of the State Capitol (see below), Iolani, which had known much turbulence in its event-packed history, was at long last vacant. The State of Hawaii wisely set about refurbishing and restoring it so that when completed it will be a museum of the monarchy. Meanwhile, the No. 1 chamber—the Throne Room—remains pretty much open to visitors. Its crystal chandeliers were brought from Europe by King Kalakaua. The thrones are replicas of the originals you will have seen in the Bishop Museum. All about are the feathered staffs known as *kahilis* that followed Hawaiian royalty wherever it moved, usually being waved by an attendant, not so much to circulate the air as to remind others present that a regal VIP was on the scene. On the palace grounds are *Iolani Barracks,* dating to 1870 and sporting neo-medieval crenelated walls; and a charmer of a *bandstand*—the Royal Hawaiian Band performs regularly—which Kalakaua had built in 1883 as his coronation stand.

Kawaiahao Church (Punchbowl and King streets) is a National Historic Landmark. And well it deserves to be. The Reverend Hiram Bingham, one of the better known of the early missionaries, was responsible for its original design, in 1837. The look is New England colonial, except that the material is native coral stone, and the belfry above the colonnaded entrance is somewhat inappropriate Gothic. The church was completed in 1842 and has more royal associations than any other house of worship in the Islands, including St. Andrew's Cathedral. It's at Kawaiahao (you pronounce every syllable, but it's still a tongue-twister) that monarchs have been christened, married and buried from. The grounds include a pair of cemeteries, both with interesting markers, as well as the mausoleum, Gothic style, in which King Lunalilo is buried, and adjacent, a one-time schoolhouse that is older (1835) than the church and is the only adobe building in town. Within Kawaiahao are a series of murals by Patric Baurenschmidt that were dedicated in 1973, and that are worthy of your attention because of their subject matter: the Hawaiian monarchy. There are no less than twenty-one of them, and they include all eight reigning monarchs, as well as their consorts and a number of their children. The church distributes a gratis leaflet describing each painting.

Pearl Harbor has been under United States auspices for more than a century. It is about as superb a natural harbor—near the center of the south coast of Oahu with a relatively narrow entrance channel leading to an enormous inner area—as any navy could want to find in the Pacific, or in any ocean, for that matter. But only with the advent of the Spanish American War, toward the turn of the century, did the U. S. Navy begin to develop it as a base. (The pearl oysters, from which the name derives, are a thing of the past.) Still, it evolved through the first four decades of this century, known virtually only to Naval personnel based there and to the locals. Then, at 7:55 A.M. on December 7, 1941, the Japanese Air Force bombed the ship-filled harbor, sinking or damaging eighteen vessels in two hours; more than 3,000 U.S. military lost their lives. The biggest ship lost was the U.S.S. *Arizona,* one of seven battleships at anchor in Battleship Row; when she plunged to the bottom, she took 1,100 of her Navy and Marine Corps crew with her. That day was President Roosevelt's immortal "Day of Infamy," and resulted in United States entry into World War II. I was based at Iroquois Point in Pearl Harbor a couple of years later, enroute with the Navy into the Pacific. And I did not return until a good quarter-century later, by means of one of the popular commercial boat tours. The time consumed is half a day, but it is time well spent. You sign up with a tour agency—I booked with Trade Winds Tours—and hop a bus in Waikiki that takes you to Kewalo Basin, between Waikiki and downtown. There you board the *Adventure V,* for the tour. Even the sail along the coast—past the impressive downtown skyline and the Aloha Tower—is enjoyable. Although you do not go ashore at Pearl Harbor, you're given a map, and a commentator —reading an intelligent commentary—points things out along the way: Hickam Field, the submarine base, Ford Island, and most important, the Battleship Row area which is the site of the U.S.S.

Arizona Memorial—a gleaming white enclosed bridge that spans the hull of the historic ship, framing a marble wall on which are inscribed the names of the military who died when the *Arizona* went down. If you like, you may take a free, Navy-sponsored launch tour of the *Arizona* Memorial—actually boarding it for a briefing by a Navy guide, on the events of December 7, 1941. The Navy runs its tours throughout the day, usually 9 A.M. to 3:30 P.M. daily except Monday. The hitch is that you must provide your own transportation to the *Arizona* Memorial Boat Landing, adjacent to Halawa Gate, at Pearl Harbor. Still another free Navy tour takes you by boat, from the same landing, for an hour's look at Navy installations—submarine base, drydocks, key piers, supply center and Ford Island, in the center of the harbor. No matter how you go: have a look at Pearl. It is not for nothing that the Interior Department has declared it a United States National Historic Site.

The Polynesian Cultural Center is a fair distance from town, up the east coast at Laie, which for many years has been the headquarters of the Mormon Church in Hawaii. The massive white Mormon Temple—first to be erected after that at headquarters in Salt Lake City—is not open to non-communicants of the church, but is worth a drive past. Laie is also the site of the Mormon-operated Church College of Hawaii, many of whose students are from South Pacific islands, where they came to know the Mormons through their missionaries. Gifted youngsters on these islands are given scholarships to the Mormon college at Laie, and from among these groups, the Polynesian Cultural Center staffs its program, with the result that it couldn't be more authentic. Some four hundred of the Church College's students are singers, dancers or otherwise employed at the cultural center. The center embraces half a dozen distinctive traditional-style villages, one each representing Samoa, the Maori culture of New Zealand, Fiji, Tahiti, Tonga and—fear not—Hawaii. At each, you'll find the student-workers—demonstrating handicrafts, preparing typical foods, singing and dancing. Additionally, there are several performances daily of a spectacular water show, Polynesian style, and still another theatrical production—different from the daytime one—each evening. Restaurant, snack bar, shop. Accessible by travel agency tours, if you like. If you are not going on to the South Pacific from Hawaii, this is as good a substitute as you're going to find in State No. 50. And if you *are* going on to the South Pacific, consider the Polynesian Cultural Center as a briefing ground; I'm speaking now not only as the author of *Hawaii A to Z,* but of *South Pacific A to Z,* as well.

Punchbowl: A volcanic crater in the foothills of the Koolau Mountains, just above Honolulu, Punchbowl is endowed with quite the most spectacular setting in town. It served as a defense fortress during the era of the monarchy. During World War II it was a fire-control post for the defense of the harbor below, and during that same time, the then Territory of Hawaii offered it to Uncle Sam as a military cemetery. A million-dollar federal appropriation made possible the construction of the National Memorial Cemetery of the Pacific, which was dedicated in 1949. Later, in 1966, the cemetery's memorial building opened. It comprises a chapel, a gallery of mural maps of Pacific World War II and Korean War battles, and a series of stairways whose marble walls are inscribed with the names of more than 18,000 servicemen missing in action. The lookout point, which is *makai,* or seaside, of the crater offers a memorable vista of downtown just below, Waikiki, Diamond Head and—appropriately enough—Pearl Harbor in the other direction. If you've never visited a U.S. military cemetery, you should. I have observed them at points around the world, and this is the most beautifully situated of all.

State Capitol: You have probably seen your share of state capitols, and you didn't come all the way to Hawaii to see another. Well, that's what *you* think. Leave it to our newest state to create our most imaginatively designed state house. The Hawaii State Capitol is a wow. Take the siting. The Capitol is downtown within the shadow of venerable Iolani Palace, which lies *makai* of it (toward the sea). Rather than raze the historic palace—which is what might have happened in some states—the planners of the Capitol placed it adjacent to the palace, allowing even the most casual of passers-by to appreciate the continuity of old to new, yesterday to tomorrow. And on the other side of the Capitol, *mauka* (toward the mountains), lies Washington Place, the Executive Mansion that is the oldest continually inhabited residence in Honolulu. Then comes architecture. At first glance, the Capitol—designed by John Carl Warnecke & Associates in collaboration with Belt, Lemmon & Lo—might appear as just another variation of the squarish, post-World War II pavilions made popular by architect Edward Durrell Stone. But that is only at first glance. Saunter up the approach walk from South Hotel Street and you see that the building configuration is at once crownlike, reminding one of the monarchy, and volcanolike, reminding one of Hawaii's volcanic origins. Then you note the sixty-foot fluted columns that encircle the structure, and you detect how cleverly they have been designed so as to evoke the Islands' palm trees. Within, the Capitol's central main-floor court is open and roofless, as befitting a tropical state house. Both sun and rain fall as they will upon the blue mosaic floor. Then note the chambers of the Legislature. Each is sensibly designed with open glass windows so that visitors may look in from the central court even if the rooms are closed and the chambers not in session. The House of Representatives has the colors of the sea and sky (blue and green) while the Senate has earth colors (reds, browns and sands); each is decorated with a striking tapestry. There are four levels. You would like to visit the governor's office. Why not? Take the elevator up, and welcome to his reception room, where a secretary offers you a gratis brochure on the building. The lieutenant governor? His offices on the other side of the building are quite as accessible. And the views from the top level are sumptuous. A tour, however brief, elates one, for few official contemporary structures anywhere in America are at once so functional and so esthetically satisfying. On the way out, pause in the central court to observe its only piece of sculpture: an unconventional—albeit extremely piercing—likeness of Father Damien, the Belgian missionary-priest who worked for sixteen years with the lepers at their colony on the Kalaupapa Peninsula of the Island of Molokai, dying himself of the disease at the age of forty-nine. The sculpture is by a young Venezuelan-descended sculptor who calls herself Marisol, and lives and works in New York. A copy of the Marisol work, along with a replica of the famed statue of King Kamehameha I in front of Honolulu's Judicial Building, are Hawaii's two entries in Statuary Hall in the United States Capitol in Washington. Wrote *San Francisco Chronicle* art critic, Alfred Frankenstein, of the Damien statue: "At the Capitol, Father Damien stands in very dark bronze. His is perhaps the only figure of them all to which one will return often as a work of art rather than as a curious byproduct of American politics."

OAHU: ALPHABETICALLY AND SELECTIVELY

I do not know a major tourist area of the globe that is more underappreciated by visitors. Your average *malihini* (newcomer) pads down at his Waikiki hotel, visits the beach regularly, takes in some of the after-dark spots, and considers himself transformed into a *kamaaina* (old-timer) if he's taken in the Kodak Hula Show and possibly Sea Life Park. All of this is fine as far as it goes. I am only making a point as regards Oahu: it need not be corny and stereotyped if you don't want it to be. It and the rest of the state have far too much going for them, as a uniquely historic and cultural Pacific crossroads, to be patronized as a kind of marine Luna Park. As the principal island of a group that made the transformation from a bucolic clutch of Polynesian tribes into a Western American state within two centuries, Oahu is worthy of the traveler at his most curious.

Alexander Young Building: Not for everyone, this Bishop Street landmark, but for those of us old enough to remember when it was downtown's fancy hotel—or at least aged to the point of recalling that during World War II it was a mostly military affair. A turn-of-century Italian Renaissance pile, it is twelve very substantial stories of what are now offices, there being no longer any demand for downtown hotel rooms.

Aloha Tower: From when it was built, in the early twenties, until the airplane came to dominate the tourist transportation scene in the early fifties, the Aloha Tower was synonymous with a Hawaiian holiday. This is where your ship tied up as the band played Queen Liliuokalani's classic "Aloha Oe," and where the hula girls draped *leis* over you neck as you alighted—or departed. To this day, you may visit the tenth-floor balcony for a super view of the city, the mountains and Waikiki. Please do.

The Aquarium, located in Waikiki's multi-attraction Kapiolani Park, seems to draw more locals than visitors. The latter seem to consider that the more time-consuming, more distant and more expensive excursion to Sea Life Park obviates the need for an inspection of the more mundane Aquarium. Possibly. Still, this is an excellent, professionally operated repository of marine life resident in the waters of the Hawaii area. Worth a look.

Beaches: Well, *Waikiki* to start. And don't knock it. It is crowded in season, but the bathers and sunners are good-natured, frequently decorous, and at all events, amusing to watch pass in review, or to watch as *you* pass in review. It is fun to promenade the length of the beach or portions thereof—from, say, the public beaches Diamond Head of the Moana all the way *ewa* past the Fort De Russy military beach, to the Hilton Hawaiian Village. The swimming is invariably very good indeed and so, for that matter, is the surfing, this being where the sport began in the days of the monarchy. Stay at a beach-front hotel and you'll see the surfies way, way out on the far waves from the moment the sun rises until it sets. *Hanauma Bay* is as good a reason as any to visit Koko Head Park at the *makai* end of Oahu's east coast. *Kailua Beach* is a broad, capacious strand, up the east coast. A

nice outing in itself, or as a refresher in the course of an exploratory tour out of Honolulu. *Kahana Beach* is a good ways up the
east coast and might well be combined with an excursion to the
Polynesian Cultural Center at Laie to the north. *Makaha Beach*
is smack in the center of the west coast. This is the site of the International Surfing Meets. Picnic grounds are nearby and so is
the Makaha Valley Golf and Country Club (Chapter 3) where
you might want to have lunch.

The Blow Hole is an Oahu natural curiosity and a near-neighbor
of Koko Head, at the foot of the east coast. You watch from your
parked car as the sea water is forced through a small hole on a
ledge of rock, with the result a veritable Yellowstone-type geyser.

Byodo-in Temple: Not the genuine article, if you would quibble.
But still a well-done replica built with great care and at great
cost, of its ancient namesake in Japan, with a great Buddha
statue, an enormous temple bell of the kind the Japanese make
magnificently, and a natural setting—it is called Valley of the
Temples Memorial Park—quite as elegant as those in the moth-
erland. The location is near Kaneohe, *mauka* from town.

Chinatown: Like a scene out of a forties movie, downtown Honolulu's Chinatown (lying between the harbor, River and Beretania
streets and Nuuanu Avenue) is a network of two-story structures,
mostly shops with exotic if not distinguished wares, dating to the
turn of the century. The most opulent exterior is that of the Wo
Fat Restaurant (Chapter 4), with tile trim and a second-story
pagoda turret. Aside from the Oriental scene—noodle shops, little
cafés, herb stores, a produce market and souvenir emporia—there
are recent additions to the scene, especially on Hotel Street—
sailors' tattoo parlors, pool halls, pinball-machine galleries, bars
and nightclubs (Chapter 5) of dubious esthetic distinction. Meanwhile, all about the area, other ethnic groups—including blacks
(yes, there are soul-food restaurants), Hawaiians, Japanese and
Filipinos—have opened enterprises.

City Hall (Punchbowl and King streets, downtown), also known as Honolulu Hale, is of the same era as the Royal Hawaiian Hotel, in Waikiki—the late twenties. It is also of similar Spanish design. Do walk in to see the splendid inner court, sans ceiling; a very grand staircase, and quantities of stonework embellished with carving executed by imported Italian artisans.

Diamond Head is the eons-long extinct volcanic peak whose elegant profile has for long been Waikiki's, if not all Hawaii's, trademark. All the sadder that authorities allowed skyscrapers to go up at its base in recent years. It marks the eastern boundary of the Waikiki area, and it is possessed of a rather spectacular crater that is easily—but rarely—inspected. There's a road leading to it, and within are some nondescript official structures of no especial import. Still, you may want to be the first on your block.

Falls of Clyde is the name of a 266-foot, iron-hull, four-masted sailing ship that was built in Glasgow in 1878, and saw decade after decade of mostly Pacific service until she was retired and, only in recent years, restored as a museum under the auspices of Honolulu's Bishop Museum. The Hawaiian association, Scottish birth notwithstanding, is a strong one, for the *Falls,* in 1898, became a part of the Matson Navigation Company. Her colors were at first Hawaiian and later, after annexation, American. At any rate, she passed her peak years as a workship—and no nonsense. The restoration tells it like it was, without an iota of glamour, as one sees from the cramped albeit spick-and-span crew's quarters. But not even the captain, let alone the other officers, lived a luxurious life. Climb aboard and see for yourself.

The First Chinese Church of Christ (1054 South King Street) is among the Oriental-influenced churches that are an architectural Honolulu anomaly. This one, a product of the twenties when the Spanish style was so prevalent, combines that motif with a pagoda-style belfry and a lonely Chinese-influenced tile doorway.

Foster Botanical Gardens: Floral *leis* and what remains of the lovely gardens of the Royal Hawaiian Hotel (they were bigger before the Sheraton-Waikiki was squeezed into the space it occupies) are for many visitors the extent of Hawaiian flora encountered. Pity, this, especially with a proper botanical garden right in the core of downtown. Allow yourself time for a walk-through that will amount to a free botany lesson—trees, vines, ferns, and the flowers of Hawaii, including orchids in abundant variety, and other gorgeous species, as well.

Hawaii School for Girls (2933 Poni Moi Road): This suggestion is no more practical than is the Punahou School (see below). Still, the visitor interested in Hawaiian history might like to have a look from the outside. Though now a private school, the building was originally known as La Pietra. It is Modified Mediterranean out of the twenties, very grand, very capacious, and pointed out so that you'll have an idea of how the wealthy descendants of the missionaries took care of themselves. La Pietra had been home to the illustrious Walter F. Dillingham.

Inari Jinsha Shinto Shrine (2132 South King Street): This one is an exotic beauty, an unabashed duplication of similar places of worship in Japan, even including the front garden, which affords just enough perspective.

The Judiciary Building, in the downtown cluster of major structures on King Street, went up about a century ago, a few years ahead of Iolani Palace, which it is sometimes mistaken for by first-time visitors in the neighborhood. Its original function was as a secretariat for the royal government, although King Kalakaua made after-dark use of it for entertaining, pending the completion of Iolani. Came the end of monarchy and it assumed its current function. The bold, larger-than-life statue out in front, with gilt trim, is of Kamehameha the Great, the unifier of the Islands. On his birthday, June 11, Honolulans drape his outstretched arms with specially-wrought Kamehameha the Great-sized *leis,* all of a dozen feet in length.

Kapiolani Park is a Waikiki landmark and has been for something like a century. It is named for the consort of King Kalakaua, the donor of the park to the municipality. With Diamond Head as a backdrop, it embraces 140 acres of playing fields, public beaches with changing facilities and life guards, a golf driving range, tennis courts, picnic-barbecue facilities, the earlier-recommended Aquarium and Zoo (of which more later), a bandstand at which the esteemed Royal Hawaiian Band gives delightful free concerts most Sunday afternoons, and the Waikiki Shell, at once the setting for the eighty-five-piece Honolulu Symphony's Summer Starlight Concerts, and of the admission-free, always-packed Kodak Hula Show; dismiss the last-mentioned as tacky if you like, but it's as good a way as any to see the Hawaiian hula properly danced—and with no cover charge. What the Kodak folks want is for you to use up as much film as possible on the dancers. And why not?

Korean Christian Church (1832 Liliha Street): In the same way that the Makiki Christian Church (see below) evokes Japan, this structure puts one in mind of traditional Korea—tripletiered, tile-roofed, with unabashed inspiration from the homeland. Have a look.

Makiki Christian Church (899 Pensacola Street) is the most striking of the Oriental churches in Honolulu. This one is a Hawaiian adaptation of the towering multi-story castles that make the traditional Japanese landscape so romantic and so sought after by visitors. Save yourself the additional trip; it's all here on Pensacola Street.

Museums are sadly undervisited on Oahu. The two most outstanding—the *Bishop* and the *Honolulu Academy of Arts*—are earlier recommended in the group of requisite attractions which is nominated as the Essence of Oahu. But there are others, also worthy of the attention of the visitor who would go beneath surface Hawaii.

The Alice Cooke Spalding House (241 Makiki Heights Drive), in the posh Makiki Heights section of town, had been the home of a daughter of one of the Big Five families, Alice Cooke, whose mother was founder of the Honolulu Academy of Arts. A wing of the house today serves as the official residence of the director of the Academy, and the rest of the structure is a branch of the Academy, whose specialties are the Asian decorative arts. Exhibits rotate, but you may be sure of seeing something special—Japanese screens, Thai stone rubbings, Korean ceramics and applied arts ranging from furniture to lacquerware. And there is a bonus, assuming you get to the house *at least 45 minutes before the scheduled closing time:* It is the three-acre garden, planted during the decade leading up to Pearl Harbor, by the Reverend K. H. Inagaki, a Japanese minister who was an absolute whiz of a horticulturist. The garden takes time—give it a full hour—because it is really ten gardens, leading one into the other. A guide booklet on sale in the house is recommended before you set off, the better to appreciate this series of botanical treats. You start with a Chinese garden, go onto a Japanese one planted with stone and metal rabbits, and before concluding have taken in a Weeping Banyan Cove and an Orchid Garden, to name a few. But even skipping the garden, you may have the view from the back porch of the house, of Diamond Head, the Punchbowl Crater and the Waianae Mountains, with the Pacific in the background. It is smashing. The rich live well in Honolulu.

Hawaii 1800 Museum: Lest it be considered a source only of crass commercialism, the Rainbow Bazaar, a shopping center in the Hilton Hawaiian Village compound, operates this commendable repository of mostly nineteenth-century Hawaiiana.

The Mission Houses Museum (553 South King Street), in the heart of downtown, is a remarkable bit of preservation that conveys in no uncertain terms how the early nineteenth-century missionaries brought every facet of their New England culture with them. The months-long journeys they undertook, via Cape Horn, and the exotic and frequently hostile culture into which they were thrust, were no detriments to them. Hawaii was to be not only Christian, but New England Colonial as regards architecture and interiors. This museum is a cluster of three structures. The main house is constructed of lumber especially cut for the purpose in the mother country and shipped from Boston in 1819. Judds and Binghams were among the illustrious missionary families who lived under its roof. There are, as well, a smaller building—the so-called print house—and a structure made of coral blocks that was originally a storehouse. The interiors are at once authentic and charming. Kudos to the landlord, the Hawaiian Mission Children's Society, who operate a gift shop and Hawaiian historical research library. Other similar museums are the Lyman Memorial in Hilo, on the Big Island; the Maui Historical Society and the Baldwin House, both on Maui.

Queen Emma's Summer House (2913 Pali Highway, in the Nuuanu Valley, *mauka* of town) is a single-story, white-frame pavilion, simply but handsomely colonnaded, and in a lovely garden of its own. It was the away-from-town retreat of the consort of King Kamehameha IV, who reigned in the mid-nineteenth century, from 1854 to 1863. The Daughters of Hawaii, who maintain and operate the house, apparently suppose that visitors know much more about the mixed-blood Queen Emma than most of us do. The amiable volunteer ladies on duty during my last visit could answer none of the basic questions I asked about the house, its furnishings or its occupant. And the only documentation offered is one side of a flier (the other is devoted to Hulihee Palace, which the Daughters operate in Kailua-Kona, Hawaii) and a few postcards. Which is something of a pity. You fail to appreciate such a lovely place without a little more background. Queen Emma was part descended from Hawaiian *alii,* or nobility, and part from the Englishman John Young, who was a top counselor to Kamehameha I. She was not only the founder of the Queen Emma Hospital—a commendable if unsurprising function for a queen—but with her husband, she founded the Episcopal (then Anglican) Church in Hawaii, even touring England to raise funds and find an architect for the construction of a cathedral—St. Andrew's in downtown Honolulu. As Dowager Queen Emma, she ran for election to the throne, following the death of her husband's successor, Kamehameha V. But she lost to King Kalakaua, and never quite forgave him—or his family, including Crown Princess (later Queen) Liliuokalani—for his victory. At any rate, within the house are a painting of the pretty young Emma, an enormous royal bed, quantities of *kahilis* (the tall feather staffs that are a principal symbol of Hawaiian royalty), a room dedicated to the visit of the Duke of Edinburgh (Victoria's second son), a slew of paintings of Hawaiian monarchs and their consorts, quantities of bibelots and some super Victorian furniture.

Schofield Army Museum: Unless you remember James Jones's novel *From Here to Eternity* and the film based upon it, or unless you were stationed in Hawaii during World War II, you may not be familiar with Schofield Barracks. It was bombed, along with the Pearl Harbor Naval Base, and it symbolizes the U. S. Army in Hawaii. Located in the interior of the island, *mauka* of Pearl, it operates a rarely visited museum, with a not inconsiderable body of historical materials that convey, for better or for worse, the role of our men in khaki, on these islands. Monday and Tuesday have been the traditional closed days, but you had better check the current schedule.

Waikiki Historical Museum: Not to be outdone by the Hilton Hawaiian Village, the Sheraton Waikiki Hotel operates this well-composed collection. It is mostly photographic, with old snaps of the bucolic Waikiki of yore. What a difference even a quarter-century has made, let alone the past hundred years! While you are in a nostalgic mood, trot next door to the base-

ment corridors of the Royal Hawaiian Hotel to see *its* elderly
photos of the neighborhood, lining the walls.

Our Lady of Peace Cathedral (Fort Street Mall), possibly because it is without monarchical associations like St. Andrew's
Cathedral and Kawaiahao Church, is relatively little known outside the Roman Catholic community. Which is not quite fair, for
it is handsomely neo-Classic, of Hawaiian coral stone, and with
a well-proportioned, column-supported portico. And, by Hawaiian
standards, considerable age; it has been on the scene since 1843.

Paradise Park: If you have to make a choice between this commercial attraction and the later-described Sea Life Park, I would
choose the latter. Still, Paradise Park, in a multi-acre setting in
the verdant Manoa Valley not far *mauka* of town is a worthy
destination, if birds at all interest you. The name of the game
here is trained feathered performers, circus-style and amusing
enough, with shows taking place regularly throughout the day.
There's a restaurant-snack bar-gift shop in connection.

Punahou School (1601 Punahou Street) is not, of course, open
to the public, but it is surely worth pointing out to the interested
Honolulu visitor that this institution's still-in-use Old School Hall
dates back to 1851, only a decade after the missionaries established Punahou for their kids' education.

Royal Mausoleum (2261 Nuuanu Avenue): The setting could
be the English countryside, save for the palm trees. This is a mid-
Victorian (1865) mock-Gothic chapel that went up during the
reign of Kamehameha V. His predecessor, Kamehameha IV was
the first sovereign to be buried there. At one point, there were
nearly twenty royal personages in the Mausoleum. Now, there are
under a dozen. You needn't stay long, which is not to say you
shouldn't go at all.

St. Andrew's Cathedral (Queen Emma and Beretania streets,
downtown) as much as any other single structure in Honolulu

illustrates the strong affinity of the Hawaiian monarchy for things British. It came about as a result of Kamehameha IV's familiarity with the Anglican-Episcopal ritual, as a result of his travels in Britain and America. Along with his equally anglophile wife, strong-willed Queen Emma, he was successful in the importation of an Anglican clergyman, who promptly baptized the Queen. The King himself translated the Book of Common Prayer into Hawaiian, and after his death off went his widow to England— a long, long journey in those days—to raise funds for the construction of a cathedral and to find an architect for the project. Kamehameha V laid the cornerstone in 1867 and in 1902 the structure was finally consecrated, later changing its allegiance from Anglican to U. S. Episcopalian, when Hawaii became American territory. (Queen Emma's association with St. Andrew's was not to be forgotten by her antagonist of later years, Queen Liliuokalani. In her autobiography, Liliuokalani minces no words at her irritation with Emma's friends, who after Emma's death, asked that she be buried from Kawaiahao, the also-venerable Congregational Church with strong royal associations. "Why," asks Liliuokalani, "supposing it had been at all necessary to select a church for her funeral, did they not select the Episcopal church? That was her own . . . and she should have been buried therefrom; for while living she had strong attachment to it, and equally strong feeling of opposition to other denominations . . .") What one sees today is a nicely sited, mostly Gothic structure which, despite its English origins (even much of the stone was imported from England), is more akin to the Gothic churches of France than to those north of the Channel. The nave and sanctuary are very handsome indeed, despite the severely jarring 1958 addition to the front of the building. It is essentially contemporary in design and frames an elaborate front wall of stained glass. The question is: why?

Sea Life Park is a scant hour's drive up the east coast, and is great fun. It is not unlike similar enterprises on the west coast, and what it does, it does very well indeed. There are a number of shows—a tank show with dolphins and penguins performing with human trainers; Whaler's Cove, with whales and their trainers giving a Polynesian-accented performance; a sea-lion feeding pool. And upon entering, one is led past a remarkable 300,000-gallon tank, inhabited by a thousand-odd remarkably visible tropical fish, representing scores of species. Shop, restaurant. Allow yourself a good half day.

State Library: The public libraries in Hawaii are a state, rather than a municipal operation. The main building, located in the heart of downtown, is essentially Spanish style. Big draws are the Hawaii and the Pacific rooms, with an extensive collection; a periodical room with daily papers from the Mainland, as well as from foreign countries; exhibits of work by the state's own artists, usually changed monthly; and a series of murals in the children's room whose theme is ancient Hawaiian legends. There is a branch—the Waikiki-Kapahulu Library—at the foot of Diamond Head, with a special shelf designated "Sand"; it's where you are kindly asked to shake the sand from those borrowed books you've read on the beach. Only in Hawaii! Not far from the Main Library, just in front of the building housing the State Attorney General's Office, is a bronze tablet in memory of Captain James Cook, the first Westerner to visit Hawaii, where—on the Big Island—he lost his life in a skirmish with locals on the beach. The marker describes Captain Cook as a "Forerunner of modern civilization in the Pacific Ocean. In Hawaii 1778–1779."

The Shingon Temple (915 Sheridan Street) went up during World War I, smallish, and the place of worship of a Japanese Buddhist sect; its elaborate roof is its handsomest feature.

Washington Place is a history-laden house—the oldest continually inhabited residence in town—with royal, republican, territorial and contemporary associations. It's the gracious, Georgian-style frame house across the street from earlier-described Iolani Palace. John Dominis, a *haole* who built it in 1874, had struck it rich in Hawaii. His son, also named John, inherited the house, and

became the husband of Crown Princess—later Queen—Liliuokalani. During the many years they made it their home, it was, in effect, a royal palace. Liliuokalani moved across the way to the
palace during her two-year reign, but returned to Washington
Place after she was deposed in 1893. She lived there for some
years thereafter, until she died in 1917, not long after which the
American Government bought the place as an official residence
for the territorial governor. It has been the Executive Mansion,
home to governors both territorial and state, ever since, and as
such the scene of official entertainments at which heads of state
from all parts of the world have been guests. You will need an invitation to get in, but no one will stop you from peering through
the wrought-iron gate to see the garden—with tree-ferns, giant
vines, shell ginger, pandanus and palm trees—and the lovely
colonnaded facade.

The University of Hawaii and the East-West Center (Manoa) are,
perhaps, more important for their functions than for their appearance. Miss a drive through the campus they share and you have
not—with respect to architecture, at least—missed a great deal;
there are no individual buildings of especial esthetic distinction.
The multi-school university is a state institution and the unique
East-West Center is partly funded by the U. S. State Department
and has students from countries throughout the Pacific basin, including, of course, the United States. There's an agreeable Japanese-style garden, and a Thai-imported pavilion built of the teak
for which that land is celebrated. Students run guided tours of both
the university and the East-West Center, and at both there are programs, performances and exhibitions that can be worth taking in.

Zoo: You have a zoo at home. Why Hawaii's? Well, there are several good reasons. The first is because it's so pretty. You wander
about in a setting of African tulips, ginger, hibiscus, monkeypod
trees, date and coconut palms, and an absolutely enormous banyan tree. And then there are the Hawaiian specialties—Hawaiian
owls, Hawaiian hawks, the Hawaiian gallinule—a local water-

bird, and most rare of the lot, the Hawaiian nene, the official state bird: a gooselike creature that had been headed for extinction. And there are a dozen or so tortoises, the propagation of which is still another specialty. For the locals, there are the lions and tigers, the giraffes and elephants, the camels and bears you know so well from home.

THE BIG ISLAND: HAWAII

Hawaii is perhaps the most curious of the major islands. It is the biggest in area by far (fully twice the size of Delaware) and it has attributes that count both for and against it, as regards its desirability as a tourist destination. The pros are a historic past richer than any of its neighbors, peaks so high that skiing is a developed sport, the remarkable Hawaii Volcanoes National Park and good deep-sea fishing. The cons are a coast surprisingly lacking in swimmable white-sand beaches, and a principal town handicapped by excessive year-round rainfall. (While Kailua-Kona, on the west coast, averages 65 inches annually, Hilo, across the island, averages 150 inches.)

The 76-by-93-mile Big Island breaks down regionally. The Kona coast, centered on the still-charming old village of Kailua-Kona, fringes the island's western and, by and large, very rocky shore, with deep-sea fishing taking the place—with some minor exceptions—of ocean bathing. Directly south is the historic area where Captain Cook landed—and was killed—and where a centuries-old sanctuary for political and religious asylum has been restored as a national historic park. The south coast, other than being the locale of South Point—the southernmost bit of the United States of America—is little more than a part of the route to the more noteworthy attractions of the east coast and its environs. Foremost of these is Hawaii Volcanoes National Park, centering in and about Kilauea Crater. To the north and east is Hilo, a not unsubstantial urban center on a pretty, hotel-flanked bay.

The interior of the island is largely taken up with its pair of monstrous mountains. Beautifully named Mauna Kea extends 13,796 feet heavenward, and you'll find skiers on its slopes weekends. Also felicitously named Mauna Loa is nothing less than the planet's most active volcano, and is just a hundred-odd feet lower than Mauna Kea: 13,680.

Due north of Mauna Kea is the Parker Ranch, No. 2 in all of the United States, after the King in Texas. The Parker is a near-neighbor of the Mauna Kea Beach Hotel. Mauna Kea's beach is what white-sand swimming beaches are—or at least should be—all about in Hawaii, or anywhere for that matter. Its plant is what tropical-resort hotelkeeping is—or at least should be—all about in Hawaii, or anywhere for that matter; it is a principal island attraction.

The Big Island, then, is for long-term vacationers if they are prepared to budget for the grand-luxe Mauna Kea or are keen for a sustained bout of game fishing off the Kona Coast. For most visitors, a few days encircling the island suffices, with headquarters either at Kailua-Kona, Hilo or Mauna Kea Beach.

The Kona Coast

Kailua-Kona Village is the Big Island's classic charm spot. The world-celebrated Kona coffee is cultivated in nearby plantations; Captain Cook landed—and was killed—just a few miles to the south; and it was here the first missionaries came ashore in 1820, only a year after Kamehameha II—the second of the united islands' kings—abolished the archaic *kapu* system, thereby removing restraints that had precluded the unimpeded reception of Western ways. The village is easy enough to walk about, with a single principal thoroughfare paralleling the coast. There are a number of heart-of-town hotels, with the Kona Hilton an eight-to-ten-minute walk from the center of the village; and several additional hotels—none, though, with proper swimming beaches—

out of town. For my recommendations in this regard, see Chapter 3. There are a profusion of shops (Chapter 7), a number of restaurants, bars and cafés (Chapter 4), and a trio of worth-inspecting historic structures on Alii Drive, the main thoroughfare. The most important is *Mokuaikaua Church,* a handsome, New England-style structure that the missionaries put up in 1837, and which has been in continuous use ever since, making it quite the oldest place of worship in the state. There is, as well, its across-the-street neighbor, *Hulihee Palace.* Only a bit newer than the church, it belies its rather grand name (it is hardly a palace, but rather a two-story, modified-Georgian house). Still, Hawaiian royalty used it for holidays, and the Daughters of Hawaii—who operate it—have filled it with agreeable Victorian-era furnishings and mementos of resident royals. Traditional open-hours do not include Sunday, so if you want to visit it, pick another day. Even though it has been modernized without a modicum of imagination, *St. Michael's Church* is important because it is the oldest Catholic church on Hawaii, dating to 1850—ten years after the first priests were sent from Honolulu to celebrate mass in the village. Outside of town, you may, if you like, visit the *Sunset Coffee Co-op* (don't expect Kona coffee to be appreciably—if any—cheaper on home ground than when it's exported), and you will want to go south to *Kealakekua Bay* where a monument—not easy to read unless you're in a tour boat—is erected to Captain Cook's memory. Nearby, and easily taken in at the same time is the *City of Refuge National Historic Park.* Not a few visitors expect an urban area and are disappointed to find quite the reverse, with a group of *tikis,* or carved wood figures, among the relatively few non-natural objects. The City of Refuge was a twelfth-century religious-political sanctuary, and nothing more. The Interior Department has restored it intelligently, and you do well to ask a Ranger for commentary, or for the gratis descriptive leaflet that will clear up your questions. Not far distant, off Route 16, is a little turn-of-century Catholic Church—St. Benedict's—whose inner walls and ceiling were covered with frescoes by a Belgian priest; thus the name, *Painted Church.*

Hawaii Volcanoes National Park

Hawaii Volcanoes National Park is the Big Island's biggest attraction. Prepare yourself for crowds and allow a good half day for this one; more if you would like, for there is an attractive hotel, *Volcano House,* with its own volcanic golf course (see Chapter 3) plop in the center of the action; you may, at the very least, lunch there, in the company of several thousand other hungry visitors. What one hears more about than anything else on the Big Island is the mythical Goddess Pele, who, according to tradition, lives in whatever Hawaiian volcano is currently in a state of eruption. Hawaiian Volcanoes National Park is, then, Pele's Park. It was first described by one of the earliest missionaries—the Reverend William Ellis—who came upon Kilauea Volcano in 1823, only three years' after his colleagues' arrival on the island. The best way to begin a park visit is to step into the *Thomas A. Jaggar Memorial Museum* at Park Headquarters, and take in the movie depicting recent eruptions, and the exhibits—including graphic relief models —which explain what the park is all about. Then embark upon the eleven-mile *Crater Rim Drive,* in the course of which you'll take in bits and pieces of the whole scene—recent lava flows, raw craters, devastated areas, undisturbed verdant jungle, lookout points like Byron Ledge and Kilauea Iki, the Devastation Trail —a boardwalk journey not unlike those at Yellowstone National Park in Wyoming—and *Thurston Lava Tube*—still another walk, this through a lushly verdant area by means of a tunnel through which had once passed streams of fiery lava.

The Hilo Area

Hilo is a pleasant town, fronting a broad, hotel-lined (albeit beachless) bay, with a neat-as-a-pin downtown, an ever-expanding branch campus of the *University of Hawaii,* the pretty Japanese-style *Liliuokalani Gardens,* a number of commercial orchid gardens open to the public (the better to have you buy) and two requisite bits of old Hilo. The first is *Haili Church,* a missionary-established New England-style structure that goes back to 1859, conducts services in both English and Hawaiian, and has a Hawaiian choir of statewide repute. The second is *Lyman House Museum* (276 Haili Street) in and of itself worthy of a Hilo visit for the newcomer curious about the history not only of the Big Island but of the entire state. Lyman ranks with the Bishop and the Mission Houses museums in Honolulu and the Baldwin House in Lahaina. The Reverend David B. Lyman and his wife, Sarah, sailed from New England to Hilo, arriving in 1832. They put up their New England-style house seven years later. It has been a museum since 1932, and at one point walls between the downstairs rooms were, unfortunately, removed. Still, this part of the house is now furnished as it was during the Lyman era, with partitions replacing the walls. It is all there as it was—papa's study, the boys' and girls' rooms with the kids' clothes, the nursery with the original cradle, a dining room, a proper Victorian parlor that contrasts with a plainer everyday sitting room, a century-old kitchen, and lots of family mementos, including a priceless photo of all seven Lyman children, and the family's treasured curio cabinet. But the house is only half of the museum. A modern museum building, opened in 1973, adjoins. Its main-floor gallery is a History of Hawaii in one easy circular sweep, beginning with early Hawaii, and continuing through the missionary era, into the Chinese, Portuguese, Japanese, Korean and Filipino immigration periods. The whole is beautifully done, with exhibits of the handicrafts and other cultural contributions of each arriving group. Hilo's *Rainbow Falls,* at the edge of town, are pretty enough. But, along with a Lyman Museum visit, it is an excursion north along the perfectly beautiful Hamakua Coast to *Akaka Falls* that should be considered absolutely requisite. The falls are at the end of Route 22 past cane fields and the sleepy village of Honomu, in the midst of a sixty-six-acre state park, so lush and verdant that you forgive the Hilo area every drop of every inch of its rainfall. The inspection is undertaken by means of a marked trail on a cleverly devised circular route with vistas of the pair of four-hundred-foot falls enroute treats. There are wild orchids, thick clumps of bamboo, brilliant growths of giant ferns at every turn. And an occasional bench, so that you may sit down and take it all in. Enroute back to Hilo, be sure and stop at the coastal town of *Onomea* for a spectacular coastal view; you look through a natural arch to the surf pounding against the rocky shore, way below.

The Kamuela Area

The little town that is the headquarters of the immense Parker Ranch is named Waimea, but it is more often than not called Kamuela, which is Hawaiian for Samuel, the first name of founder Parker. What you want to see in Kamuela, besides the *paniolos* or cowboys themselves, are *Imiola Church,* New England style like so many in Hawaii, and dating back to 1857; the *Parker Ranch Tourist Information Center,* which regularly throughout each day shows a quarter-hour film on the history of the ranch; and the center's two museums. *The Parker Museum* is chock-a-block full of early Parker and museum mementos, while the *Duke Kahanomoku Memorial Museum* is a repository of the trophies, medals and other awards given to a noted Hawaiian athlete-hero. There is, as well, the *Kamuela Museum,* where the highlights are exhibits of Hawaiiana, both early-day and from the period of the monarchy. But what you want to aim for is ranch life—*paniolos* at a calf-branding are not difficult to come upon. *Mauna Kea State Park*—with trails for hikers wanting to gain the summit, is in the neighborhood. So is *Pololu Valley Lookout,* at the end of Route 27. There is a fine white-sand beach, with changing facilities and picnic tables at *Hapuna Beach State Park,* and last but hardly least there is *Mauna Kea Beach Hotel* (Chapter 5), which should be taken in if only for one of its delicious buffet lunches, or at the very least a drink and a look at this beautiful hotel's beautiful public spaces.

THE ISLAND OF MAUI

I have never been much of a partisan for popularity contests; still I have the suspicion that in a poll of all-round Neighbor Islands, Maui might come out the winner. If any one island beyond Oahu is the very essence of Hawaii, all wrapped up within a 120-mile shoreline, this is it.

Maui was the capital of Kamehameha I, the strong sovereign who united the islands, and its port-town of Lahaina remained the capital for the reigns of the two succeeding Kamehamehas. As if that were not enough, the very same Lahaina was the battle-ground—perhaps that is too strong a term—for the inherently antagonistic philosophies and practices of strong-willed puritanical New England missionaries and the crews of whaling vessels out to relax with the local ladies after many long months at sea. If Maui cannot equal the Big Island as regards the possession of active volcanoes, it surpasses it—in at least one inspector's view —with the magnificent spectacle of an easily viewed dormant crater called Haleakala that in and of itself is designated by the Department of the Interior as a National Park. Add this quartet of additional ingredients essential to the success of tropical tourism: splendid white-sand beaches in abundance, a climate that is not hampered by excessive moisture, a perfectly lovely countryside of verdant variety. The still relatively little-visited east remains serene as of old. The west is the very-put-together Hawaii of today, and perhaps of tomorrow. In the center, is the splendor of volcanic Haleakala.

Maui is the second largest of the islands, after Hawaii, and the perspective visitor should be prepared to give it some time. Even disregarding relaxation days—for this is first-rank beach territory —a good three or four exploratory days are not too much.

Geographically, Maui is best considered as two-part, east-west oblong—one great eastern sector, this with Haleakala occupying much of its core, and a smaller isthmuslike western chunk, with a pair of towns at midpoint between the two.

There are three commercial airports, one west, one east, and one toward the center. It is this last—Kahului Airport—that gets the lion's share of inter-island traffic. It is named for, and adjacent to one of the twin-towns, with neighboring Wailuku and the scenic Iao Valley just next door. The most-visited sector of the island embraces a portion of the northwest coast, and the combination could not be more felicitous: historic Lahaina and the next-door beach resorts of Kaanapali and Napili, with smaller resorts farther south on the west coast, in and about the town of Kihei. Haleakala National Park is easily gained either from the west coast resorts or, in many instances, directly from Kahului Airport, for in-a-hurry visitors. There remains eastern Maui—a comfortable half-day drive from Kahului along the north coast to the stubbornly old-fashioned village of Hana. Here are highlights:

The Twin Towns

The Twin Towns are more often than not *terra incognita* to the Maui vacationer who whizzes from the airport to his Kaanapali or Napili hotel and doesn't give this part of the island another thought until it's time to return to Kahului Airport. Well, resorts *Kahului* and *Wailuku* are not (even though the former has several bay-front hotels; see Chapter 3). But they do constitute urban Maui—agreeable small towns that convey what Neighbor Island living is all about to the 40,000 or so permanent residents of the island. Kahului is essentially a transport town—the airport, of course, and with Maui's principal commercial harbor. Wailuku is the Maui county seat and aside from the expected official buildings—county administrative machinery, court house and the like —there are several destinations for the newcomer curious about the island's past. The *Maui Historical Society* (Iao Valley Road) calls home a rambling mid-nineteenth-century missionary house with the double-story verandas typical of the architecture of that era. Hale Hoikeike, as the place is called in Hawaiian, is an eminently visitable repository of objects not only of the period when the capital was at nearby Lahaina, but of earlier—and later—times as well. Recommended for the history buff who would like a perspective other than that afforded by Lahaina. Also, it is off the beaten tourist path and is usually refreshingly uncrowded. Note, too, the *Iao Congregational Church,* just opposite. There's an old high-spired church, *Kaahumanu* by name, that the missionaries erected in 1837, the second decade after their arrival. And then I call to your attention, also, the Hawaiian Room of the main *Maui County Free Library;* the collection is rich with materials relating to the island's background.

Easily combined with a Twin Towns tour is the pretty Iao Valley. Drive but a few miles west of Wailuku, and you see how it got its name: From the *Iao Needle,* a freak of nature that protrudes some 2,250 feet into the atmosphere.

Kaanapali and Napili Beaches

Kaanapali and Napili beaches are the neighborhoods that most Maui visitors call home. Kaanapali is Maui's Gold Coast—a three-mile stretch embracing a handful of beachfront hotels (Chapter 3)—the island's most luxurious. Whalers Village is a honey of a shopping-eating-drinking-center with museum overtones (Chapter 7). And there are, as well, a pair of golf courses, including the super-special 18-hole Royal Kaanapali, created by Robert Trent Jones, the Tiffany of golf-links designers. All of the other accoutrements of resort living are present—excellent tennis, marine activity, a substantial variety of places to eat very well indeed (Chapter 4). Distances between hotels are not so great that one cannot walk—going via the beach is my favorite way. There is a free, inter-hotel shuttle-bus service as well, although one must be prepared for erratic schedules with at times excessively long waits, when taxis must sometimes be called to one's rescue. Lahaina is less than five miles distant, so that taxi fares are not exorbitant, and one has the option to employ the

only surviving railroad in the state—the Lahaina-Kaanapali &
Pacific, if you please; it's fun. Nearby Napili Beach appears to
attract your more experienced Hawaii vacationer; the traveler
who has done all of the islands and wants to settle down to a
quieter, more settled kind of holiday away from the tour groups,
in a setting quite as agreeable in its way as splashier Kaanapali.
Napili's small but charming public beach—Fleming's—is one
of the most inviting on the coast.

The Kihei Area

Considerably south, in and about the neighborhood of the little
town of Kihei, a mixed-bag resort area is developing. The coast
line is pretty, the places (Chapter 3) tend to be on the smaller
side, with a fair share of condominiums operated as hotels, and
the price level is mostly moderate.

Lahaina

Lahaina is west Maui's magnet town, and has been since the
start of the nineteenth century, when in 1802 Kamehameha I
made it his capital—the first seat of government of the united
Hawaiian Islands. (Or at least most of them. The only major
island not in the group then was Kauai, not conquered until
1810.) Royal patronage—especially important during the pro-
ductive reign of Kamehameha III (1825–54)—was not all
that Lahaina was to enjoy. Within a decade or two, both the
missionaries and the whalers converged upon Lahaina. When
the Arctic ice began to cover the north Atlantic, the whales
swam south, into the harpoons of the rapidly growing whaling
fleets. The men spent many months at sea, and when they got to
Lahaina they wanted a rip-roaring good time, the while pro-
visioning their ships and considerably enriching the town's economy, if not its moral stature. The need for whale oil came to
an end before the Civil War, by which time Lahaina had known
four fast, furious and prosperous decades of whaling. As many

as fifty ships anchored in its waters simultaneously, and one year—1859—saw a grand total of 549 ships visit the port.

The pity is that much of old Lahaina—like so many of the older appurtenances of the continental United States—were allowed to disappear over the years. Only relatively recently, did a group of concerned local citizens mobilize their resources in the privately funded Lahaina Restoration Foundation. Working with the state-subsidized Maui County Historic Commission they are making progress in bringing back as much of the old Lahaina as there is to be refurbished. The current situation, with respect to inspection by visitors, boils down to being a case of more than most visitors allow time for, but less than many preservation-oriented visitors expect.

Lahaina is best seen leisurely, and on foot. Give yourself a good half day, preferably starting in the morning, when it's cooler and fresher, and staying on in town through lunch. Arm yourself, straight away, with the excellent free brochure published by the Maui County Historic Commission entitled *Lahaina: A Walking Tour of Historic and Cultural Sites*. You'll note from its map that the town's core is compact and uncomplicated, most of the old places in and about the harbor and Front Street—the main thoroughfare fronting the Pacific. Start out with the Lahaina Restoration Foundation's pride and joy, the carefully restored *Baldwin House*. This was the white-stuccoed two-story veranda-faced home of the Reverend and Mrs. Dwight Baldwin, built of coral stone after their arrival from New England, via Waimea—down the coast—where they spent their first few years. Trained as a physician at Harvard as well as a minister, Dwight Baldwin typified the missionary at his best. His history-filled house, aside from sheltering the Baldwins and their six kids, was home to an almost interminable guest flow, ranging from Hawaiian *alii* to whaling-ship captains. Along with the Lyman House in Hilo and the Mission Houses in Honolulu, the meticulously restored Baldwin—replete with furnishings ranging from Dr. Baldwin's sextant to the crib used for all the children—is essential to an understanding of the not inconsiderable impact of the missionary on

Hawaiian life. Next door, is the one-time *Masters' and Mates' Reading Room,* now a bookshop and the headquarters of the Lahaina Restoration. It was originally established by the missionaries as a quiet spot where ships' officers could read and write letters home. Still another Foundation enterprise is the *Carthaginian,* an 1850-style whaling vessel with its interior, including crew's and officers' quarters, much as it would have been when the ship spent long months at sea. Also in the core of town, in and about a giant banyan tree that is well over a century old, are the turn-of-the-century, still-very-much-in-use *Pioneer Inn* (Chapter 3) and the *Courthouse,* dating to 1858, where the Hawaiian flag was replaced by the Stars and Stripes on Annexation Day in 1898, while the townspeople sadly sang "Hawaii Pono'i." Not far away, are *Hale Paahao,* the prison where both locals and visiting sailors—particularly the latter—were incarcerated; *Hale Pa'I,* the printing plant where the missionaries produced both religious and lay materials, mostly after translating the originals into the Hawaiian language; and a variety of houses of worship including the new *Buddhist Shingon Temple* and the older *Episcopal Church* (built in 1927 to replace the original dating to the mid-nineteenth century); *Maria Lanakila Church,* a 1920s replacement of an original Roman Catholic structure that was built more than a century ago; and *Waiola Church,* a 1953 successor to an old church that first went up in 1828, just after the missionaries arrived.

Haleakala National Park

Haleakala (pronounced *Ha-lay-ah-ka-la* and meaning House of the Sun, in Hawaiian) is the supreme Maui experience. Indeed, I would not quarrel with anyone who termed it the supreme all-Hawaii experience. Even the getting there—the distance is thirty miles from Kahului—proves to be a memorable drive, with the departure from near sea level, and the not-so-gradual change in temperature, not to mention terrain, as one ascends. Haleakala is a volcano that has not erupted since 1790 but that could—the National Park Service believes—erupt again. Its gargantuan crater—three thousand feet below its rim—is a mass of vari-colored cinder cones and wildly formed lava flows, the lot about equaling the area of Manhattan island. As you make the latter part of the climb from sea level, the views—given clear weather—are as fine as can be had anywhere in the state. It is not only the immediate vistas of cane and pineapple, it is of the islands in the distance. If you're lucky, you find yourself taking in Lanai and Molokai and little-known Kahoolawe, not to mention the summits of Mauna Loa and Mauna Kea on the Big Island, even before you reach the park proper, from a couple of lookout points along the way. By that time you are readying yourself for the first official park point, the Visitor Center where rangers are on hand to answer questions and distribute the well-written free National Park Service leaflet on Haleakala. Let me add here that Donald F. Ruhleg's illustrated *Haleakala Guide* is first rate and a recommended purchase. If you think the vista from the Visitor Center is spectacular, you must reserve judgment until you move along to the structure called Red Hill Visitor Building, way atop the mountain, and directly overlooking the crater. The front wall of this building is one vast picture window; a map of the crater explains just what it is you are looking at below.

You will take pictures, you will buy post cards, and if you're like me, you will take notes interspersing exclamation points throughout your scribbles. Because the view is matchless. You are looking down at the entire, miles-long length of the crater, and if you find yourself wanting to get closer—as do many visitors—you are going to have to do so by means of your own feet, or a horse, or a combination of the two. There are some thirty miles of well-marked trails into the crater, several sites for tent camping, and a number of simple campers' cabins (Chapter 3). Allow at least a day for substantial walks, or as much as three or four days for more elaborate treks. There are very brief walks along the rim, too. As you move about, look for the park's specialties. One is flora—the unique silver-sword plants—found nowhere but at Haleakala and protected by law. They appear part tree, part flower, part cactus, and blossom only once in their four- to twenty-year lifetime. And the other is fauna, if you can call the Hawaii State bird fauna. This is the rare, and at one time nearly extinct, nene, a kind of goose, except that it's better looking than our domestic variety, with mostly gray feathers and a white neck.

Hana and the East

Old Maui hands will tell you you don't know Maui until you've experienced Hana. An airport of its own or no, you had just better make the drive across Route 36 from Kahului, because getting to Hana is considerably more than 50 per cent of the adventure. A half day is enough time, assuming you can steel yourself to not make a stop at pretty-appearing points along the way; make no mistake, there are many. The last half of the fifty-odd-mile journey is about as scenic as you'll find in the state—narrow, curvy, occasionally rutted road notwithstanding. What we're talking about here is one sublime vista after another—seascapes, verdant glades, sparkling waterfalls, crystal-clear pools fairly inviting you to brake the car and dive in. The flora is lush too—mangoes, mountain apples, guavas, ferns, tropical blossoms in abundance. There are some lovely picnic spots; and if you will be ambling leisurely, take a picnic lunch along, for the only public restaurant is the dining room of the Hotel Hana Maui (Chapter 3) at journey's end—and then only at specified meal hours.

Have a map of Maui with you and consider stops enroute at the Rinzai Buddhist Temple; a venerable hamlet called Lower Paia that gives the impression of having seen better—or at least more prosperous—days, a Zen temple and graveyard at Kuau; a bamboo forest, waterfalls and picnic area at Waikamoi; the 1860 churches in the typically Old Hawaii villages of Keanae and—farther along the road—Wailua; the inviting picnic grounds —to the sound of cascading water—of Puaa Kaa State Park; and still another state park closer to Hana called Waianapanapa, where the draws include a pair of caves and a black-sand beach.

Hana itself—quiet, friendly, plain as an old shoe but much prettier—lies at the foot of a hill with a huge cross atop it, from which you want to get the view. There are places to stay (Chapter 3), a general store with wares so diverse that it is known throughout the state, and—beyond town—a number of excursion points, most especially the Seven Pools at Kipahulu, where one pool leads to another lower-down one, with the ocean at the farthest extreme, the lot superbly swimmable and an enchanting setting for a picnic lunch.

THE ISLAND OF KAUAI

First, the pronunciation. Or pronunciations. You are correct if you say it Cow-*ay*-ee. But Cow-*aye,* in two syllables, is acceptable too. As for the island itself, it is quite the most spectacular of the lot—with gorgeous beaches, deep and verdant valleys, a canyon that compares in majesty with the Grand on the Mainland, incredible vistas from just about wherever it is you happen to be, and a central mountain range that has the dubious distinction of being just about the wettest patch of terrain in the world. Not for nothing is Kauai—created by a single immense volcano—the oldest-in-time of the inhabited islands in the group.

As if all of this natural distinction were not enough, Kauai has other attributes. It was the first of the Hawaiian group to be settled by the Polynesians from the south. It was the first island to be visited by the intrepid Captain Cook. And it does not let its sister islands forget that it was the political hold-out of the chain, the very last to go along with King Kamehameha I and join the united Hawaii; that happened in 1810—just a decade before the missionaries came to the Islands from New England—when Kauaian King Kaumualii yielded his realm.

Tourism came later to Kauai, at least to any appreciable degree, than to the other major islands. It is the fourth largest of the Big Seven both in area (627 miles) and in population (about 31,000). Which is not to say that Kauai is any more a Pacific paradise than its neighbors. It tends to cloud over a bit more than one always likes and can be dampish and coolish, powdery white beaches notwithstanding. And for the urbanist, it is quite the quietest of the major islands. One is not left thumb-twiddling in the bigger hotels after dark. Nothing like that. It is just that even when compared with the Big Island or Maui—forgetting the fleshpots of wicked Waikiki—the ambience of Kauai is the most bucolic of the lot. Which is just what many vacationers seek. But not all.

Given the natural features of the island, it should come as no surprise that sightseeing is more developed a pastime than on any other Neighbor Island. The Kauai folks have it all down pat on their bus and limousine tours. According to the amount of time at one's disposal on this near-circular island—with its sole town of consequence and its airport in the southeast—you divide your rubbernecking into either two parts or three. The former is seg- mented into essentially a northern and southern swing. Not that you can't go off on your own for the kind of leisurely exploring that is the most fun. Assuming you haven't come to relax for a week or two—and Kauai has many such repeat customers—you will want a bare minimum of two full days for basic inspection of the island. But for comfort and relaxation, I would double that, as a minimum. Advance homework? Before you arrive, try and make a mental list of all of the movies you can remember with Polynesian settings. Chances are, they will have been filmed on Kauai. You'll hear all about them from Kauaians, a high pro- portion of whom know precisely what scene from what film was filmed on what part of what beach, and with what actors playing what roles.

Lihue

Lihue, the Kauai county seat is attractive, friendly, well- scrubbed-and-manicured, and with a two-building museum—the *Kauai Museum*—vastly more substantial than one would expect in so small a community. The most popular exhibit, called "The

Story of Kauai," is at once a historical, geographical and cultural history of the island, with everything from a graphic contour map showing the hills and valleys to a diagram of Waimea village as it might have looked to Captain Cook and his crew when they went ashore almost two centuries ago. There are exhibits relating to the early Hawaiians and the early missionaries, the later immigrants and the later cattle ranches. An interesting shop (Chapter 7) is operated in conjunction. Lihue's Public Library is nearby, as is a substantial shopping center (Chapter 7) and buildings housing county, state and federal offices.

The Lihue Airport, the only commercial airport on the island, is just outside of town. There are two principal batches of Kauai hotels. The larger group is a few miles north of the airport in and around Wailua, while a smaller group is to the south, at Poipu Beach. Still another hotel, the important Kauai Surf, is at Kalapaki Beach, nearer to town and airport than either Poipu or Wailua.

Selected Kauai Destinations

What happens on an island as small as Kauai, where sightseeing is the major newcomers' diversion, is that the tour guides latch on to relatively minor attractions, work them into their spiels, and ballyhoo them to the point that if you don't perceive a rock formation vaguely resembling what might be in the shape of Queen Victoria's profile, you can—if you let yourself go— become convinced that you haven't seen Kauai. What follows, therefore, are one appraiser's idea of the most significant destinations on the island.

Waimea Canyon

Waimea Canyon is to Kauai what Haleakala National Park is to Maui and Hawaii Volcanoes National Park is to the Big Island. This should be your single most urgent destination. The location is north of Waimea, the historic point at which Captain Cook went ashore a couple of centuries ago, on the south coast.

The canyon is something like a mile wide, some ten miles in
length, and nearly 3,700 feet deep. The canyon's colors—like
those of the Grand Canyon—change, depending upon the time
of day—earth tones, golds and beiges, become deep purple and
blues and greens. The approach to the canyon's principal lookout
points is via its spectacular Rim Road, where I suggest you relax and take in the vast panorama, moving on, if you like to
nearby Kalalau Lookout, so that you'll have an idea of the many
faceted splendor of the Kalalau Valley, some four thousand feet
below.

Fern Grotto

It's Hawaiian tourism at its unabashed corniest. Still, you want
to go. What happens is that at the mouth of the Wailua River,
you board a long covered boat, where you and scads of fellow
passengers are crammed into narrow, uncomfortable wooden
seats. The Captain, who is going to take you up the river to the
grotto, is likely to be a good-natured, multi-talented youngster
who wears four hats—pilot, banjoist (he steers with one hand
while strumming with the other), singer (this activity is accom-
plished simultaneously with the first two) and tour guide, this
last including commentary while aboard his vessel and also ashore,
going to and from boat to grotto. In high season, the pilgrimage
from shore to sanctuary (and sanctuary is no exaggeration for
Fern Grotto is the scene of frequent local weddings) is apt to
take considerable time, for the means of egress is single file, and
the crowds can be fierce, numbering in the several hundreds.
Upon arrival at the grotto, which puts me in mind of the great
stage of Radio City Music Hall—all in natural rock, of course—
the captain-singer-banjo player-tour guide explains things and
moves everyone to a certain spot, the better to appreciate the
natural acoustics. After which, the single-file exodus is undertaken, and the vessel reboarded for the return journey to the
mouth of the river.

Hanalei Bay

Hanalei Bay is a perfectly beautiful spot smack in the center of the north shore. Its beaches—the film *South Pacific* was partially shot there, and you will be told precisely what scenes—are sublime, and the view inland of taro patches in the Hanalei Valley way below is pure picture postcard. Not only that, but enroute, you pass by *Kilauea*. Its lure is a photogenic lighthouse, with an absolutely enormous lens, set atop a precarious cliff that attracts some unusual bird life. I find the birds' names of interest; there are Great Frigate birds, Red-footed Boobies and White-tailed Tropic birds, among others. You see a lot else that you like as you travel about Kauai—sugar fields, gardenia bushes, grapefruit orchards, a lovely botanical garden called Ola Pua, and country churches, not the least of which are the ultra-mod St. Sylvester's (Catholic) and the nicely mellowed Christ Chapel (Episcopal).

THE ISLAND OF MOLOKAI

Molokai has not had an easy time of it—for a long, long time. Ancient Hawaiians, not averse to visits—warlike or otherwise— to neighboring islands, tended to steer clear of Molokai for its priests had a reputation—not necessarily justified—for powers of evil. Indeed, Molokai's visitors, for the most part, during those days before the united Hawaiian monarchy, were the occasional escaped outcasts from one of the other islands.

Kamehameha the Great conquered Molokai toward the end of the eighteenth century, just a few years after journeying there, for the first time, to take the hand of a Molokai princess in marriage. But little more than half a century later the reigning monarch was faced with the problem of dealing with the victims of a disease that is believed to have come to Hawaii along with its Western visitors: leprosy. Kamehameha IV's government set up a leper colony on the isolated Kalaupapa peninsula of Molokai. It might never have been better known than any other similar institution had it not been for the labors of a Belgian missionary priest, Father Damien de Veuster.

When leprosy was still a universally feared and dreaded disease, and long before there were any effective medications to control it, Father Damien moved into the settlement, bag and baggage, with a program that blended compassion with practicality. He was only forty-nine when he died of the disease himself, although not before having been recognized for his work. Father Damien, though not Hawaiian-born, is surely the greatest man Hawaii has produced. It is to the state's credit that he was the subject of the only work of sculpture designated for the splendid new State Capitol. And that, moreover, a copy of that sculpture is one of the two pieces Hawaii—like every state—is allowed at the Capitol in Washington.

Oblong-shaped, close to forty miles long, and with more than its share of fine peaks and broad valleys, Molokai has never made it as a tourist destination. The stigma of the globally known leper settlement has been a lot for it to live down. And as if that were not enough, here is a Hawaiian island that is virtually devoid of swimmable beaches.

The result is that Molokai's five thousand-odd residents mostly make their living through the Islands' extensive pineapple industry; Dole and Libby, McNeill & Libby are the big operators. There is some farming and ranching, and the principal visitors are generally permanent residents of the other Hawaiian islands who want to get away from home for a few days, without going far. For the casual Mainland visitor uninterested in inspecting the leper colony, there seems little point in a Molokai visit.

Visiting Kalaupapa

The regularly scheduled, competently operated half-day tours of Kalaupapa, constitute Hawaii's best-kept tourist secret, even though they have been a part of the Molokai scene since as long ago as 1957, by which time the settlement had begun a gradual phase-out, with most patients considerably helped by modern drug therapy. It was in that year that the Hawaii State Health Department ruled that the general public (except for kids under sixteen) could visit the Hansen's Disease colony on authorized guided tours. What is essential to know before undertaking such a tour is that the Kalaupapa Peninsula can be reached only by air from the Molokai Airport, or by a time-consuming hike over a difficult trail, or by also-time-consuming muleback, in special tour groups run by Tropical Rent-a-Car, Molokai. The casual visitor's big question is: Can you fly over to Molokai early in the morning, connect with a local plane to Kalaupapa, and fly back after the tour, to the Molokai Airport for an air connection back to Honolulu that afternoon? The answer is yes, but you must plan in advance; be sure to depart Honolulu early enough in the morning to make a flight via Brandt Air (a local Molokai carrier using small craft) to Kalaupapa. Or, you may fly Royal Hawaiian Air Service direct to Kalaupapa from Honolulu. It is only at Kalaupapa that one may join the tour. It embraces the village where the settlement's remaining patients—a reported 145, all in arrested states and all ambulatory—live and work, the Catholic, Protestant and Mormon churches, and the separate Kalawao area. This was the portion of the peninsula—at once beautiful and beautifully situated—where the colony had its beginnings. Here, the lures are the best known of the island churches built by Father Damien—and like the others, small but handsome—and the original Damien grave. Tour members are asked to bring box lunches; these are eaten in the picnic area—high above the sea and with a splendid view of the mountains sweeping straight into the Pacific—after the tour concludes. Ask all the questions you like of the guide, and take pictures freely, except of patients. The tour operator is Damien Molokai Tours, Box 1, Kalaupapa, Hawaii 96742.

Elsewhere on Molokai

The island's other diversions, beyond the earlier-mentioned hunting and fishing, are limited. The most essential relates to

Kalaupapa. It is the view afforded of the peninsula, and a good bit else of the island, from a well-situated belvedere in the interior of the island, called Kalaupapa Lookout. Still other island highlights have Kalaupapa associations. These are the churches around the island erected by Father Damien; they include Our Lady of Sorrows (1874) and St. Joseph's (1876). Both are white-framed and tall-steepled, charming Victorian Gothic in style. St. Joseph's has an old photograph of the priest over the altar, with this simple legend: "Father Damien, 1840–1889. Apostle of the Lepers," while Our Lady of Sorrows, restored in 1966, has a Damien statue.

Molokai's sole metropolis is the tiny town of Kaunakakai, with a movie theater, several shops and restaurants, an attractive high school, and not far distant, riding stables and the 9-hole Iron Hills Golf Course. Hotels (Chapter 3) are out of town.

THE ISLAND OF LANAI

It would be an exaggeration to say that Lanai—the sixth in size of the islands after Molokai and pronounced La-*nye*—is one vast pineapple plantation. But a whopping big chunk of this 18-by-13-mile island is Dole country. Even though Captain Cook was an early visitor, there are not many followers in his footsteps—to understate. Like Molokai, Lanai's chief appeal is to Hawaii residents who want to get away from it all for a couple of days.

Aside from views of the vast plantation fields—the Doles bought the island in 1922 for $1,100,000—there is not a great deal else to divert one. Except—in the case of serious hunters—quantities of deer, wild sheep and goats, and game birds like partridge and pheasant. Unlike Molokai, smaller Lanai has respectable swimming at adjacent Holupoe and Manele bays. And still another strand—Shipwreck Beach—where the remains of ships tossed ashore long ago still are to be seen. Boats may be rented for good deep-sea fishing—the esteemed *mahimahi,* swordfish and tuna being the most common species. There is a 9-hole golf links and a solitary hotel (Chapter 3) that overlooks the solitary town where most of the island's 2,600 residents live. It is called, sensibly enough, Lanai City, and its pretty, garden-encircled Congregational church makes a nice contrast to the severity of the iron-roofed houses. The altitude—some 1,500 feet—makes for an agreeably coolish climate, and the terrain gives an atypical north woodsy look to the place, thanks to great clumps of Norfolk pines.

3

Hawaii to Stay

SETTING THE HOTEL SCENE

There are two generalizations that may be made about the extraordinary Hawaiian hotel plant. The first is that nowhere—in no resort area of the globe of which I am aware—is cleanliness closer to godliness. Hotels in Hawaii, regardless of category, absolutely shine. (And godliness is not to be taken for granted either; every Hawaiian hotel is blessed by a Hawaiian minister at its dedication, no matter the religious conviction, or lack of it, of the proprietors. This blessing is taken very seriously indeed, and so is the selection of the clergyman for the job. A hotel that is not sent on its way properly, in this regard, is not given much chance of success.) The second generalization is that, by and large, rate scales of hotels in Hawaii are the least expensive of any major resort area anywhere in the world of which I am aware. Hawaiian hotels give value received, be they luxury, first class or budget.

Moreover, service standards tend to be high. The visitor industry is a no-nonsense major income earner. It is big business, and most Hawaii residents know it is big business. As with the price scale, so with service: I know of no major resort area where service is consistently as friendly, or to qualify a bit, where service is any more friendly. The smile quotient is high. Which is not to say that service is always skilled, always prompt, or always cheerful. The smaller hotels frequently station young people at reception desks who have no business there, know next to nothing about their work, and are preoccupied with whatever it is kids in Hawaii are currently preoccupied about. In places that are busy—the bigger hotel coffee shops at breakfast, for example—it is going to take a while to be served in Hawaii, as anywhere. But by and large, staffs of Hawaiian hotels are good-natured, willing, and much more often than not, proficient.

There are a great many places to stay. On the Island of Oahu the Waikiki area alone has well over a hundred hotels—Maui is No. 1 among the Neighbor Islands, with some seventy hotels. Hawaii follows with about half a hundred, and Kauai trails, with some two-score choices.

ABOUT THE HOTELS IN THIS BOOK

I have approached hotels in Hawaii in this book in much the same way as I have tackled Western European hotels in *Grand Tour A to Z: The Capitals of Europe,* Soviet and eastern European hotels in *Eastern Europe A to Z,* and the hotels of other areas of the planet covered in the A to Z series. The first key word is *selective.* These are a select group which I found worthy of space in this volume, for one reason or another. The second key word is *personal.* These are hotels in which I have lived, eaten, drunk, or at the very least, thoroughly inspected.

The hotels are presented *alphabetically,* by island, and each is designated as either *de luxe, first class* or *budget.* The designations are my own, based upon my evaluation of facilities in relation to rates. In this connection, it is worth noting that the minimum rates of most de luxe hotels are not very different from the top rates of the first-class hotels, which can make the de luxe places good buys if one is able to get minimum-rate accommodations. (Specific dollars-and-cents rates are not given because they change so often: travel agents have them, or write directly.) As for the budget hotels, what makes them good buys, by and large, are kitchen facilities. Invariably, they are equipped for cooking, which makes them especially popular with couples and families who come from the Mainland for several weeks, or even several months, and are, therefore, able to prepare their own meals whenever they like, and do not feel—as do many of us—that it's not a true vacation when you must do your own marketing, cooking and washing up.

SELECTED OAHU HOTELS

Of the half a hundred hotels I have chosen for Hawaii's major island, all but a handful are within the bounds of Waikiki; one of these is just over the border, a second is a few miles distant and the last two are some distance away. Waikiki is described earlier (Chapter 2), but let me repeat here that it is the section of the city of Honolulu that fronts its own beach on the Pacific, extending from Diamond Head on the east, to the Ala Wai Yacht Harbor on the west, and running from the ocean, inland to the Ala Wai Canal. What we are talking about is an area roughly two and a half miles long and a half to three-quarters of a mile wide. The core of the Waikiki Beach area, with the biggest concentration of hotels, lies between Saratoga Road and Lewers Street on the *ewa* (or west), and Liliuokalani Street, on the Diamond Head (or east). This area contains five of the eleven beachfront hotels, and a great number of other hotels of all sizes and categories, inland from the beach. It is, not surprisingly, the beach that is the principal criterion for room rates. Hotels on the beach are generally the most costly. Rooms in those hotels facing the sea are the highest priced, with the rates rising concurrently with the floor locations. As you move away from the beach, rates tend to lower, although they can remain substantial in the cases of rooms that have ocean views, or better yet, that afford panoramic vistas of, say, the beachfront skyline and/or Diamond Head. Let me make clear that the interior of Waikiki—going *mauka* (toward the mountain) from the sea—is a delightful area. Streets are quiet and beautifully maintained with flower-filled gardens. One may walk the area at any time of day or night. And if one stays in central Waikiki, walking is the preferred means of getting about. After all, one is rarely in all that much of a hurry on holiday, the exercise is healthy, and it's fun to people-watch enroute to beach, shopping, restaurants or after-dark action. For that matter, even the extremities of the area—at hotels like the Hilton Hawaiian Village going toward downtown, or the Hawaiian Regent going toward Diamond Head, are by no means too distant for ambles into the center, either via the beach during the day, or along Kalakaua Avenue in the evening. As for chain operations, there are several. Sheraton dominates the scene, with five Waikiki hotels (as well as the Sheraton-Maui and the Sheraton-Kauai—all Japanese-owned albeit Sheraton-operated) and makes it easy for guests staying in one to use the facilities of the other four; you simply sign your name and the room number and the name of the hotel you're staying in. There are a pair of Hiltons—the Hawaiian Village operated by Hilton Hotels Corporation (the domestic Hilton organization which also has the Kona Hilton on the Big Island) and the Kahala Hilton, a part of the world-wide Hilton International group. Western International operates the Ilikai, while the Americana chain runs the Ala Moana. Hyatt is a-building, and Holiday Inns is among the motel chains represented. There are a number of Hawaiian groups, as well. Amfac, one of the original Big Five of the Hawaiian economy, is now well into the hotel field, with Oahu's Waikiki Beachcomber and eight hotels on the Neighbor Islands. The Outrigger group embraces the Waikiki Outrigger and a number of other similarly named hotels. The Cinerama chain has the Reef and a pair of neighbors. Hawaiian Pacific Resorts operates the Kaimana Beach and several other hotels, while Allen-Pacific runs a quartet of smaller hotels; and there are others.

Here are my selections—de luxe, first class and budget—presented alphabetically.

The Ala Moana Hotel (410 Atkinson Drive) is a splendid skyscraper, just between Waikiki and downtown, overlooking the Ala Moana Shopping Center (Chapter 7), and the steps-away Ala Moana Park with its own beach and tennis courts. There is a capacious chandelier-illuminated lobby, 1,300 good-looking rooms all with *lanais* (try and get as high up as you can for those views of Waikiki and/or downtown), and The Summit, a roof-top restaurant with dancing (Chapter 5), not to mention a twenty-four-hour coffee shop, separate steak and Japanese restaurants, and the festive Hawaiian Hut, with splashy South Seas shows, and late-late hours disco dancing (Chapter 6). Skilled Americana Hotels management. *De luxe.*

The Aloha Surf Hotel (444 Kanekapolei Street) is a modern structure of no especial esthetic distinction (its lobby is something of a decorative error) with a nice location between Waikiki beach and the Ala Wai Canal. What makes it interesting are those of its rooms—the Superior category they call them—that have bath and *lanai* as well as full kitchenette. Pool and bar-lounge. *Budget.*

The Breakers Hotel (250 Beach Walk) embraces a low-slung cluster of two-story pavilions surrounding a pool, near Kalia Road and not far from the beach, or in the other direction, Kalakaua Avenue. The lure here is a well-equipped kitchenette with every room or suite; these vary in size and look and those on the ground floor right near the pool might be a little noisy. Good for couples or families (kids must be over eight) who want to economize on restaurant meals by cooking. Most agreeable management. *Budget.*

Coco Palms Apartment Hotel (2465 Koa Avenue) appears to cater mostly to mature couples interested in good value for stays often running through some weeks. There are both one-bedroom suites and studios, all with bath and all-electric kitchens and kitchenettes. No restaurant, bar or pool, but the beach is a short walk away. *Budget.*

The Colony Surf Hotel (2895 Kalakaua Avenue) is a tall white skyscraper that is among the small group ruining the profile of Diamond Head, which is just behind. What redeems this place for me is a restaurant (Michel's—see Chapter 4) that is one of the best in the state. The lobby is disappointingly tiny, but the bedrooms can be extra-big and handsome (when they are, they are inaccurately called "suites" because they have kitchens, although bedroom and living room are a single chamber). There are smaller rooms, twin-bedded, and also with kitchenettes. All have *lanais*. And the beach is at the door. The neighboring *Colony Surf East* is a sister-hotel, and a good bit less expensive. *De luxe.*

The Dar Lanai Apartment Hotel (245 Kaiulani Avenue) is a smallish, simple place that is nice for older couples wanting to stay a while. Each unit comprises bedroom, living room, fully equipped kitchen, TV and *lanai,* and is big enough to sleep five. It's all spotless and the management is kind and congenial. *Budget.*

The Halekulani (2199 Kalia Road) opened up in the early thirties. It's one of the oldest hotels in Waikiki, along with the Moana and the Royal Hawaiian. The look was appropriate from the start—beachfront, low-slung and unpretentious, embracing a main building with lobby and restaurant, and a group of satellite pavilions with the guest rooms. Over the years an affluent, conservative clientele has developed, to which the hotel continues to cater, and in whose eyes it can apparently do no wrong. Still, it became apparent to me, on several recent visits—including one to the cocktail lounge and another to the restaurant—that the charm of the place was diminishing, along with the proficiency of the service, the plant (the cocktail lounge, for example, wants brightening and refurbishing), and, most regrettably, the warmth of the welcome. *De luxe.*

The Hawaiian Regent (2552 Kalakaua Avenue) is among the newer of Waikiki's luxury hotels—and an absolute dazzler. From the outside, the look is sleek. Then one views the smashing lobby —long and low and understated and leading into a lushly planted tropical courtyard. The elevated, ocean-view pool terrace, dotted with green plants and white trellises, is a beauty. The bedrooms, all with *lanais,* making good use of wicker and chrome, with bamboo-patterned wallpaper, are knockouts. There's a dilly of a coffee shop; a groovy, late-hours disco—The Point After (Chapter 5)—a smart lobby cocktail lounge, and a restaurant called The Third Floor—after its location—that is worthy of additional comment in Chapter 4. And lovely service, all combining to make one's stay so agreeable that the fact that one must cross the street to get to the beach becomes relatively inconsequential. *De luxe.*

The Hilton Hawaiian Village (2005 Kalia Road) is the epitome of the self-contained resort. The guest rooms occupy a cluster of gleaming skyscrapers, the newest of which—Rainbow Tower—has become a Waikiki landmark with its rainbow-tile design extending down the surface of a side wall. There are no less than a quartet of pools scattered about, although I prefer the beach—wonderfully calm waters for swimming and lots of white sand for tanning. Restaurants, bars and lounges run a wide gamut. So does entertainment—Polynesian revues, *luaus* on the beach, sails in the hotel's own catamaran, dressy dinners and disco dancing. And there's an elaborate shopping center (Chapter 7) that draws people from all over town. The Village is fun. *De luxe.*

The Holiday Inn (2570 Kalakaua Avenue) is a contemporary tower overlooking—but not directly on—Waikiki Beach that should be much more attractive than it is. Comfortable and with full facilities, to be sure: restaurant, coffee shop, snack bar, pair of lounges-cum-entertainment, pool-side bar, even room service. But hardly with style or charm, at least in one observer's view. *De luxe.*

The Holiday Surf Apartment Hotel (2303 Ala Wai Boulevard overlooking the canal) is a no-nonsense economy place, with studios and one-bedroom apartments, all with kitchen facilities and TV, albeit no pool, restaurant or bar. Very simple indeed, but clean and adequate. *Budget.*

The Holiday Isle Hotel (270 Lewers Street, at Kalakaua Avenue) is a contemporary heart-of-Waikiki house. Every one of the smartly decorated rooms has a *lanai* and refrigerator. There's a pool on the second floor, a popular bar-lounge, with entertainment, called Shipwreck Kelly's and a moderate-price steak restaurant. The standard-category rooms are good buys. An Island Holidays hotel. *Budget.*

The Ilikai Hotel (1777 Ala Moana Boulevard) is among the best of the biggies—thirty stories embracing 750 exceptionally spacious rooms and suites (most with kitchenettes), and public spaces that include roof-top tennis courts, a unique front yard of a mall, with shuffleboard, a putting green, nightly traditional-style torch ceremonies, and music under the stars. A ramp leads down to an adjacent lagoon beach. There are two pools, and an outside elevator takes one to the Top of I, for lunch-cum-view, or dinner dancing (Chapter 4). Other Ilikai eateries include Arthur's—among the smarter restaurants in town—and the moderate-price Chart House, as well as a coffee shop, not to mention a convenient lobby grocery-wine-liquor store. The location is super. Waikiki is a short walk away. And nearby Ala Moana Shopping Center is in the opposite direction, with downtown just beyond. A Western International hotel. *De luxe.*

The Ilima Hotel (445 Nohonani Street) fronts a pleasant street near the Ala Wai Canal and has an unglamorous lobby, to be sure, but this modern hotel offers more than at first meets the eye. All of its rooms have completely equipped kitchens as well as *lanais*. There's a pool and sun deck, but no breakfast is served (you make your own), the only restaurant being an Italian one serving lunch and dinner and not actually a part of the hotel. Friendly staff. *Budget.*

The Imperial Hawaii Hotel (205 Lewers Street) is a mod good-looker—400 rooms all with *lanais* and color TV. There's a pool and sun deck on the roof, and a variety of places to wine, dine and make merry—the Aquarium Lounge, Captain Nemo's Disco, a Japanese restaurant, and a coffee shop open round the clock; central location too. *First class.*

The Kaimana Beach Hotel (2863 Kalakaua Avenue) must share the blame with the earlier described Colony Surf and Colony Surf East—its neighbors at the foot of the mountain—for botching the silhouette of Diamond Head, near whose foot it is situated. The Kaimana's most important attribute is its beachfront location. There is an ocean-view terrace at which breakfast, lunch and drinks are served, and two restaurants, one of them Japanese. Views from the rooms can be super. A Hawaiian Pacific hotel. *First class.*

The Kahala Hilton (5000 Kahala Avenue) is quite detached from Waikiki, on its own splendid 800-foot beach in the fancy Kahala residential quarter of Honolulu. A California architectural firm—Killingsworth, Brady and Sutter—designed it in the mid-sixties, and neither Honolulu—nor the hotel's guests and visitors —have stopped talking about it. (The visitors include quantities of the understandably curious who come out on Trade Winds Tours' shuttle-buses from Waikiki to have a walk-around, and a drink or a meal.) Along with Waikiki's Hawaiian Regent and the Mauna Kea Beach Hotel on the Big Island, it is quite the most exemplary example of contemporary hotel design—both exterior and within —in Hawaii. Considering its munificence, it is not all that big: 372 rooms and suites, including the low-slung 70-room Lagoon Terrace section, wrapped around a dolphin-inhabited pond, and on the scene since 1969. The Kahala, thanks to David Williams' interiors as well as the building itself, is at once bold and of this very moment, with just enough restraint to immediately distinguish it from run-of-the-mill-modern. The beautifully proportioned lobby sets the tone, with chandeliers embellished with thousands of bits of Italian glass, not unlike the beach glass that washes ashore just outside. The bedrooms are oversized, with double-baths that have become a Kahala trademark, and *lanais* that mostly afford sublime vistas. The pool-beach-dolphin-pond area is casual, with a single, nearly alfresco restaurant doubling both as coffee shop and nighttime show locale (Chapter 5); the Maile Restaurant is among the best in the state, and the subject of comment in Chapter 4. The modish Kahala Mall shopping center, with its restaurants (Chapters 4 and 7) is a neighbor, but I must make clear that Waikiki is several miles distant. The Kahala is for vacationers who want quiet, light-touch luxury at a quarter-hour's drive from the action. *De luxe.*

The Kai Aloha Apartment Hotel (245 Saratoga Road) is low-profile, small, unpretentious and well-located, with sensibly priced kitchen-equipped studio units. *Budget.*

The Kalia Inn (2164 Kalia Road) is middling-sized modern, conveniently situated near the beach, with compact but comfortable rooms with *lanais,* a pool, restaurant-bar-lounge, and attractive tabs. *Budget.*

The Kuhio Hotel (2345 Kuhio Avenue) is smack in the center of Waikiki with the Ala Wai Canal, International Market Place and beach all convenient. This is a full-facility house—380 capacious rooms with *lanais,* pool-terrace, around which drinks and free *puu-puus*—that's Hawaiian for canapés—are a cocktail-hour habit (Chapter 5), 22nd-floor bar-lounge gained by exterior elevator; other restaurants, too (Chapter 4). *First class.*

The Kuhiolani Hotel (2415 Kuhio Avenue) is more interesting looking outside than in—with a sloping, futuristic facade. Still, rooms all have kitchenettes and *lanais.* And the price is right. No pool, restaurant or bar. *Budget.*

The Kuilima Resort Hotel and Country Club (Kahuku, Oahu) is indisputably self-contained—500 rooms in a Y-shaped structure straddling a peninsula of its own, with a big beach, an 18-hole golf course, tennis courts, pool and attractive accommodations all with *lanais.* The hitch is the location at the northern tip of Oahu, easily an hour's drive from town. Given the geography, one can see why Kuilima appeals to convention chairmen who don't want to lose their members at meetings, as well as travelers well known to the public and anxious for a restful retreat. A Del Webb hotel. *De luxe*.

Makaha Inn & Country Club (Waianae, Oahu) reposes in solitary grandeur among the green hills, in the Makaha-Waianae area of the west coast, a good hour's drive from Honolulu. The lure is golf—there is a 36-hole course. There are tennis courts, too, and Makaha Beach is less than a mile distant. Full hotel facilities with the rooms occupying a clump of two-story pavilions. *De luxe*.

The Malihini Hotel (217 Saratoga Road) is a cinder-block affair, with kitchens a part of all of its 30 studios and one-room apartments, and outdoor patio space. Nothing fancy, but with a welcoming management and a good percentage of repeaters among the mostly mature clientele. No restaurant, bar or pool, but the beach is close. *Budget*.

The Marine Surf Hotel (364 Seaside Avenue) is a sleek skyscraper filled with 120 studio units, each with kitchen, two double beds, *lanai* and color TV; roof-top pool and Matteo's Italian restaurant downstairs, from which neither breakfast, lunch, nor room service is obtainable. Among the nicer, better-looking of the new economy-class places. *Budget*.

The Moana Hotel (2365 Kalakaua Avenue) is Waikiki's oldest. Its white-frame, central section went up in 1901, and the concrete side wings enclosing it are 1918 additions. The area framed by these wings and the beach—and shaded by a giant banyan tree— has long been one of Waikiki's most beloved watering spots. Indeed, the Moana, not unsurprisingly, is Waikiki's most beloved hotel, with me among its most ardent fans. I first knew the place during World War II, when on Sunday liberties from Pearl Harbor my Navy mates and I would splurge and have the full-course

$1.50 dinners in a restaurant that now sees service as a reception-briefing-information center for groups of Japanese tourists. The hotel has been under Sheraton auspices for some years now, and I had the opportunity to live in it on a recent visit. The rooms have all been nicely updated. There is a post-World War II wing next door, all of whose rooms have *lanais* and are air-conditioned. The hotel's sole restaurant is in this Diamond Head wing (although there is a passage leading to Sheraton's luxurious Surfrider Hotel, next door *ewa* side, and its coffee shop and restaurant). However, the Moana lobby has been sadly let go. And there are two other points that should be made: The rooms of the original building are not air-conditioned. In the winter months the evenings are cool enough so that air conditioning is not essential. But, the windows must, of course, be kept open for ventilation, and therein lies the catch. Every evening of the week, save one, the later-described Banyan Court is—or at least, has been for some years—the setting for a Polynesian revue interspersed with live music for dancing. The noise, from cocktail hour until about midnight is devastating in all of the rooms of the original building, which explains why their rates are as moderate as they are, given the beach location and the famous name of this house. There is no noise though in the air-conditioned rooms of the Diamond Head wing—where windows may be closed—and at all other hours of the day the Moana is a pleasure. But if you choose the original building, plan to spend every evening on the town, or take earplugs. All that said, I still love you, Moana. *First class.*

The Outrigger Hotel (2335 Kalakaua Avenue) is also known as the Waikiki Outrigger to distinguish it from its confusingly named satellite Outriggers, all of which are less expensive. No. 1, to which we now refer, is tucked—just barely—into a Waikiki Beach location between the Royal Hawaiian and the Surfrider hotels. It is unexceptional architecturally, or as regards lobby and public-room decor. The lures are the 550 bedrooms, all with mini-refrigerators and coffee-making apparatus, color TV, and *lanais,* from many of which the views are spectacular. There is a pool, the beach at the door, and an exceptionally wide variety of places to eat, drink, spectate and dance. *De luxe*.

The Outrigger West Hotel embraces a Surf Wing (actually a separate building) and a Kuhio Wing (across the street); they are both on Kuhio Avenue, which is midships Waikiki. The Outrigger West's Surf Wing, which I have inspected, offers good value in its mostly smallish rooms, all of which have kitchenettes, *lanais* and TV. Neither breakfast nor room service is available, but Rudy's Italian restaurant is on the premises. *Budget*.

The Pacific Prince Hotel (415 Nahua Avenue) is the former Royal Prince, and now the flagship of the Allen-Pacific group of small, budget-priced hotels. There are 125 units, all with kitchen facilities. Sister hotels are the nearby, similar-type *Pacific International, Pacific Islander* and *Pacific Kuhio,* all bookable from the chain's office in the Pacific Prince. *Budget*.

The Park Shore (110 Kapahulu Avenue) is just *mauka* of Kalakaua Avenue, at the Diamond Head end of Waikiki. This is a nicely got-up contemporary house, with a range of accommodations. All rooms have *lanais*. Mid-category ones have refrigerators while top-range ones have color TV and, in some cases, kitchenettes. Like neighboring hotels, popular with Japanese groups. Depending on your room, *Budget or First class*.

The Princess Kaiulani Hotel (120 Kaiulani Avenue) becomes the "P.K." to you, as to the locals, within minutes of your checking in. It's Sheraton's only non-beachfront hotel in Waikiki—a pair of handsome towers embracing more than 1,100 rooms just across the street from Sheraton's Moana and its beach (which P.K. guests are invited to use). Rooms—decorated with winning wallpapers and textiles—are among the better looking of the Sheraton accommodations, which is saying a good deal. You may breakfast from a bountiful buffet around the pool (which I like) or in the perky coffee shop; there are, as well, both a

Japanese and a Chinese restaurant (Chapter 4) and out on
Kalakaua Avenue, one of those Sheraton Minute Chef counter
places, at which the outdoor lines are to all intents and purposes,
interminable. The princess for whom the hotel is named was the
heiress presumptive to the Hawaiian throne, when the monarchy
was overthrown during the reign of the princess' aunt, Queen
Liliuokalani. *First class.*

The Queen Kapiolani (150 Kapahulu Avenue) is at the Diamond Head end of Waikiki among the group of hotels that
cater heavily to Japanese visitors. This is a late-sixties house,
named for the consort of Kalakaua, the last reigning king, with
an elaborate lobby, upstairs pool-sun deck, nice rooms most—
but not all—with *lanai,* alfresco coffee shop, fancier proper restaurant and—my favorite—a congenial cocktail lounge that serves
delicious platters of hot *pupus* with drinks (Chapter 5). A Hawaiian Pacific hotel. *First class.*

The Reef Hotel (Lewers Street at Kalia Road) is one of those
relatively rare Waikiki hotels that is directly beachfront. The
lobby is one absolutely enormous shopping arcade, with the silver-
haired lady clients, in the company of obedient husbands, buying
as though there were no tomorrow. There are a slew of places to
eat, drink and be amused (Chapters 4 and 5). The *lanai-*
equipped bedrooms are comfortable and many offer superb views.
And the service is cheery and agreeable, given the heavy traffic.
First class.

The Reef Lanai Hotel (225 Saratoga Road) is a fairly substantial high-rise, sheltering good-value units, mostly ample-sized,
all with *lanais;* the apartments with separate bedrooms and
kitchens are worth investigating. Restaurant, bar. *Budget.*

The Royal Hawaiian Hotel (2259 Kalakaua Avenue) is Spanish
Mediterranean twenties, in the best sense of that term. It was

completed in 1927 when tourists were mostly well-heeled and came mostly by Matson ship with bulging steamer trunks packed for winter-long stays. During World War II, when I first knew the Royal, Waikiki was considerably more bucolic, albeit military-populated. Indeed, the Royal was a Navy base. Sailors and marines in from Pacific battles were honored guests in its rooms, while all Navy personnel in the neighborhood were welcome to swim at its beach and drink its beer. The Royal lost some of its lovely gardens when the Sheraton-Waikiki went up next door, in the sixties. But it is still beautifully sited and it is still—thanks be to the Sheraton folks who run it with tender, loving care—beautiful. A great long gallery, running lengthwise, is the show-place part of the lobby. There is a casual restaurant (Chapter 4) fronting the beach—a fine choice for buffet breakfast, or for lunch or dinner even if you're not a Royal resident. And the nighttime Monarch Room (Chapter 5) is a Waikiki institution. Guest rooms are traditional-style, quite as spacious as you would imagine. There is a quite super tower wing out of the sixties—coral-hued like the main building and, though contemporary in line, a handsome complement to the old original; its duplex suites are zingy. And, in the basement, whose corridor walls are hung with priceless photos of earlier eras, is the super-duper Royal Door Spa. *De luxe.*

The Sandcastle Hotel (2375 Ala Wai Boulevard) has one of the neatest-looking facades in town—sandstone, not unsurprisingly. Within, the accommodations are functional, quite attractive and most have *lanais*. There are a tiny pool, restaurant and bar on the premises. Good value. *Budget.*

The Seaside Lanai Apartment Hotel (334 Seaside Avenue) consists of something over half a hundred studio and one-bedroom apartments, well-equipped with kitchens and *lanais*. Functional if not fancy, and well maintained by a kindly, efficient management. Couples and families coming to Hawaii for the winter usually rent by the month (there are daily and weekly rates as well) with the place usually fully booked by late autumn. Don't let the tiny lobby put you off; this is a winner in its class. *Budget*.

The Sheraton-Waikiki (2255 Kalakaua Avenue) is a 31-story, 1,700-room giant, smack in the heart of the Waikiki action, with groups and conventions a specialty; lively and boldly designed public areas—surely the most heavily trafficked of any such in the state—that embrace a clutch of exceptionally attractive, imaginatively conceived places to eat, drink and be merry (Chapters 4 and 5); and guest rooms and suites—all with *lanais* and many with magnificent vistas—that are at once good-sized and good looking. *De luxe*.

The Surfrider (2353 Kalakaua Avenue) is a striking, Sheraton-operated skyscraper directly on Waikiki Beach, adjacent to (and connected with) the next-door Moana, another Sheraton property. The big news at the Surfrider are the 430 big bedrooms. They're among the most generous-sized on the beach, with two-part baths, very attractive and all with *lanais*. Get a high-up one and a postcard view is assured. I especially like the Surfrider's restaurants—an indoor-outdoors coffee shop that's nice at breakfast, when a buffet is featured, and the Ship's Tavern (Chapter 4). *First class*.

2465 Kuhio at Waikiki Apartment Hotel (2465 Kuhio Avenue) is a functional high-rise all of whose units—studio, one bedroom and two bedrooms—have fully equipped kitchens and *lanais*. No pool, restaurant or bar, but, if you please, *saunas* for both men and women. Good buy, this. *Budget*.

The Waikikian Hotel (1811 Ala Moana Boulevard) is wedged between the towers of the Ilikai and Hilton Hawaiian Village hotels, at the *ewa* edge of Waikiki. It embraces a central A-shaped lobby building, with both a conventional tower—and more to the point, a group of four, Polynesian-design two-story pavilions, whose rooms are traditional in style, with overhead fans (as well as air conditioning), louvered doors leading to their *lanais,* and casual albeit tasteful furnishings. These garden rooms are the ones to head for—cheaper than the high-rise and what distinguishes this hotel from its neighbors. There is a pool, a restaurant overlooking it (Chapter 4) and an absolute honey of a lagoon beach, with the main Waikiki strand a stroll away. A charmer. *De luxe.*

The Waikiki Beachcomber (2300 Kalakaua Avenue) is heart-of-the-strip, but not quite beachfront. It's an attractive high-rise, with tasteful public spaces that include Don the Beachcomber's Restaurant, a good-value coffee shop, the Bora Bora Room with its Polynesian shows, and a pair of bar-lounges. The bedrooms are comfortable, spacious, nicely furnished, and all with *lanais;* get a front, higher-up room and you've a super view. Astute, courteous Island Holidays Hotels management. *First class.*

The Waikiki Resort Hotel (2460 Koa Avenue) is a nineteen-story high-rise with 310 capacious, comfortable *lanai*-equipped rooms and an immense lobby, with a rather gaudy second-floor restaurant and pool-sun deck. The landlord is Korean Air Lines, and the value—especially for the standard and moderate-rated rooms—is sound. *Budget–First class.*

The Waikiki Surf Hotel (2200 Kuhio Avenue) is one of a trio of economy-class hotels under the same management and in the same neighborhood. The others are the *Waikiki Surf East* (422 Royal Hawaiian Avenue) and the *Waikiki Surf West* (412 Lewers Street). All have small pools, but no restaurants. The accommodation is clean, modern and compact, but hardly elegant; all of the rooms and apartments in the East and West buildings have kitchens; only some in the Mother House are so equipped. *Budget.*

The White Sands Hotel (431 Nohonani Street between Kuhio Avenue and Ala Wai Boulevard) is a case of last but hardly least. This is surely the most stylish and tasteful of the economy-class hotels, at least of the many in Waikiki that I know: a handsome, three-story structure that wraps itself around an inner garden, centered by a pool, with umbrella-covered tables, scattered about, and chaise longues for sunning. The 95 rooms are decorated in earth colors, with a Japanese touch. Each has a complete all-electric kitchen, and a *lanai* gained by sliding *shoji*-screen-type doors. No restaurant or bar. Congenial and competent management. *Budget*.

SELECTED BIG ISLAND HOTELS

Kona Coast

If you are going to the Kona Coast, it seems to me, you go to get the feel of the old village of Kailua-Kona. Recent years, however, have seen the construction of a number of hotels some miles south of town, in an area of the island that cannot even compensate with proper bathing beaches. My selections, therefore, are all in Kailua-Kona, with one special exception, a unique get-away-from-it-all resort, barefoot style, that has good beach swimming.

The Hukilau Hotel (Kailua-Kona) is an unglamorous oldie with, apparently, a loyal repeat clientele. It's smack in the heart of town, high enough so that you can see the bay. There are a pool, restaurant and bar. But, please understand: nothing fancy. *Budget*.

The King Kamehameha-Kona Hotel (Kailua-Kona) is one hotel (the Kona) evolving out of the site of another (the King Kamehameha), with the setting downtown (if one may so term it) Kailua-Kona, and the special attribute of a real honest-to-goodness white-sand beach—a rarity in this part of this island.

The old King Kamehameha (which may have entirely disappeared by the time of your visit) never won a beauty contest, but it was congenial, and if its Marlin Room seafood restaurant is still operating when you arrive, do go for dinner. The new Kona Hotel, consists of a good-looking pair of 230-room blocks, with a bay-view trio of restaurants including a coffee shop, and a shopping mall. The beach is a considerable enlargement of the pioneering King Kamehameha strand. The management is Island Holidays. *De luxe.*

The Kona Hilton (Kailua-Kona) ages gracefully. Not that it is old, or even elderly. Still, I have been back several times since I covered its official opening in 1969, and I still like the look of the place, especially the stairwaylike front facade of the main building. The 450 bedrooms—all with *lanais*—in all three buildings are bright, gay and imaginative. There's a nice pool, and nightly entertainment, a small beach, and grounds so lovely that there are guided tours, there being 180 species of plants, flowers, and fruits—all of them catalogued in a gratis brochure. Good eating is a Kona Hilton tradition (Chapter 4). And the location is ideal—you're a seven- or eight-minute walk from the center of the village. *De luxe.*

The Kona Inn (Kailua-Kona) is a Kona landmark; it's been around something like half a century. Recent years have seen it updated, and with an across-the-street annex added. Rooms—they total 222—are attractive but not all of them are very big and not all have *lanais*. Restaurant, bar, two pools (the smaller of the two at the annex, the other fronting the sea) nightly entertainment. *First class.*

The Kona Sunset Motor Hotel (Kailua-Kona) is a rambling single story, cement-block complex with 25 rooms, non-air-conditioned, pool, restaurant and, I gather, a devoted following of returnees who like the simple life. Kind management. *Budget.*

Kona Village Resort (eight miles north of Kailua-Kona) is an isolated cluster of some seventy thatched structures—done in the styles of the various Polynesian and Melanesian cultures—Samoa, Fiji, Tahiti, New Hebrides, Tonga, the Maori of New Zealand, and Old Hawaii. They are all on stilts and situated at random points—in the gardens, on the beach, facing a lagoon—of this delightful self-contained resort. South Seas motif notwithstanding, all accommodations have modern private baths. Meals are served in a variation of a New Hebrides long house. There are beach parties and *luaus,* and evening entertainment in still another atmospheric structure. This is the lazy life, completely informal, with facilities for deep-sea fishing and hunting, a fine pool and, most important to the serious barefoot vacationer, an honest-to-goodness, crescent-shaped beach. *De luxe.*

Hilo Area

The Hukilau Hotel (33 South Banyon Drive) has an agreeable, casual ambience, beginning with a lobby whose walls are lined with Tongan tapa cloth. There's a pool situated in an inner courtyard, and the bedrooms—especially the high-up ones from whose *lanais* there are good views—are welcoming. So is the restaurant-bar. Same management as the Hukilau in Kailua-Kona, but considerably more inviting. So far as I can ascertain from my investigations, the best economy-class hotel in town. *Budget.*

The Hilo Bay Hotel (437 Banyon Drive) is an Old Hawaiian-style hotel in a pretty garden setting with pleasant rooms, good-looking restaurants, bar-lounge and a pool overlooking the bay. Hospitable management. *First class.*

The Hilo Lagoon Hotel (101 Aupuni Street) is a biggie—421 rooms—that specializes in group business. There's a large lobby with a nice buzz to it, a variety of eateries and well-equipped rooms with tiny *lanais.* A Hawaiian Pacific hotel. *First class.*

The Naniloa Surf Hotel (93 Banyon Drive) offers bay views from many of its 388 attractive, *lanai*-equipped rooms, and is full-facility. By that I mean there's a variety of restaurants and bars including a coffee shop and night club, as well as a bay-front pool. An Inter-Island hotel. *De luxe.*

The Orchid Isle Hotel (211 Banyon Drive) is medium size. Its 117 rooms tend to be attractively furnished with *lanais* and color TV. There are a pair of pools, a restaurant (Chapter 4) with Polynesian entertainment every evening, and a bay view. *First class.*

The Polynesian Pacific Hotel (175 Banyon Drive) is about as simple as one might reasonably want. There are 13 rooms, most of them doubles. There's also a small pool, and the setting is bay-view. For the ultra-economy-minded. *Budget.*

The Travelodge (120 Banyan Drive) greets one with a modest little lobby, a surprise after the substantial look of the building. But the 146 rooms are ample-sized, attractively furnished and with *lanais*. There's a nice kidney-shaped pool with chaise longues surrounding it, and a good restaurant-bar (Chapter 5). *First class.*

Volcano House (Hawaii Volcanoes National Park, south of Hilo) is a novel idea for an overnight stay. It's right on the rim of Kilauea Crater. There are 37 inviting rooms, all with bath, and many with exciting views of the crater. Cozy bar-lounge, as well, and a dining room that feeds hundreds upon hundreds of park-tourists during the day, but that is considerably more intimate for dinner in the evening. And golfers note: there's an 18-hole course minutes away operated in conjunction with the hotel—4,000 beautiful feet above the Pacific. A Brewer hotel. *First class.*

Waiakea Resort Village (400 Hualini Street) is Hilo's charm spot, and quite one of the most imaginatively conceived hotels in the state. There have been and are other Polynesian-type hotels.

Waiakea is special in that it is, or at least gives the impression of being as much water-born as it is tropical-verdant. But first things first. Talk about planning: The absolutely lush plantings were all undertaken a full eight years before the place opened in 1973. The village proper embraces ten principal three-story pavilions. You walk to all of them, but still there is water all about, not to mention waterbirds. A rather saucy goose is likely to greet you in the reception building when you check in, and if he likes you—he took a shine to me, on a recent stay—he'll be present when you check out. There are swans, as well, both black and white, ducks galore, and the plants and flowers are brilliant. Guest rooms—there are nearly 300 but the place seems intimate—run to rattan furniture with nubby upholstery. There are no elevators (ask for a ground floor room if stairs are not for you). All rooms have *lanais,* most overlooking waterfalls and waterways. The duplex suites are opulent; some include a *sauna* and a fully stocked wine-cellar, with the guest given the key and an invitation to drink all he likes. The principal restaurant (Chapter 4) is one of consequence, and there are a Polynesian show room, coffee shop and Japanese restaurant. Operated in conjunction with the village is a honey of a shopping center called Market Place, which is detailed in Chapter 7. The staff, decked out in variations of red, blue or yellow-check uniforms, are perfectly delightful, which you perceive immediately upon arrival. Check-in is undertaken in easy chairs in the reception lounge, as you relax with a complimentary Waiakea Swizzle, offered by one of the beautiful sign-in hostesses. A Brewer hotel. *De luxe.*

Kamuela Area

Mauna Kea Beach Hotel (Kamuela): When Hawaii achieved statehood in 1959, state authorities—in an effort to decentralize tourism beyond Waikiki to the Neighbor Islands—asked Laurance Rockefeller to create a hotel at a site he liked. He picked the Kawaihae coast of the Big Island. And the result was a hotel named for the eternally snow-capped volcanic peak that dominates that region of the island. The main building is surely one of the finest designs of Skidmore, Owings and Merrill. Public spaces are decorated with a thousand-plus museum-caliber objects collected throughout the Pacific, both the South Seas and the Asian mainland and the subject matter both of a recent album-type book (which you may buy) and of an unillustrated catalogue (which is gratis). But always the ambience is of the quiet, tasteful Rockresorts kind, with the natural environment dominant over all other aspects of the scene. The word "beach" in the hotel title means just that: a magnificent crescent of white sand, backed by palms, that is unsurpassed on any of the islands. The guest rooms are the most beautiful of any in the small but choice Rockresorts chain that extends to Wyoming, Vermont and Puerto Rico. What I most enjoy in them is the service of breakfast. A cart is wheeled out to one's *lanai,* and on it appears one of the hotel's couple of hundred two-slice electric toasters; you plug it in and make your own toast, so that it's fresh and hot when you eat it. Detail like that is the kind of thing at which Rockresorts excel. There are a trio of restaurants, one relatively recent, another an elevated beachfront terrace whose delicious buffet luncheons are famous throughout the state. The 18-hole Robert Trent Jones-designed golf course is superlative, with a gorgeous ocean view (these Jones courses are a Rockresorts specialty). There are no less than nine tennis courts, and the Parker Ranch is nearby for riding under the tutelage of *paniolos*—Hawaiian cowboys, these—if you like. Not a few Mauna Kea guests visit the Big Island because of Mauna Kea, rather than vice versa; indeed, there are those who fly all the way out to Hawaii to experience this hotel. They cannot be faulted; it is one of the great ones. *De luxe.*

SELECTED MAUI HOTELS

Kahului

The Maui Beach Hotel's big A-frame lobby-restaurant-bar is its trademark. The public spaces are ample and include an upper-deck pool-sun deck. Bedrooms are comfortable. Probably one's best bet for a stay in the Kahului-Wailuku area. A Hawaiian Pacific hotel. *First class.*

The Maui Palms Hotel, though with a bay-front location including a pretty garden-cum-pool setting and restaurant facilities, is quite plain and is primarily for consideration by the limited-income traveler, and then only if he is able to book a minimum rate room, which puts the hotel into the category of *Budget.*

Kaanapali Beach

The Kaanapali Beach Hotel is the least expensive of the blue-chip group in this area, and a special favorite of the locals— which is invariably a recommendation. Though hardly barefoot-casual, it has the most informal ambience of the lot, despite an easy-to-take garden, a palm-encircled pool and a sizable chunk of beach. The bedrooms all have *lanais,* and the best bargains of the lot are not the minimum-rate ones—though naturally these are solid enough value—but the so-called suites which are, in effect, enormous combination living-bedrooms, with pullman kitchens. Restaurants here include a 24-hour coffee shop, steak house, and all-purpose main dining room. Nightly entertainment and dancing. Fun. *First class.*

The Kaanapali Plantation is a condominium-apartment-type resort, located *mauka* (toward the mountains) of the Royal Kaanapali Golf Course, affording quite splendid views of the beach-front hotels and the sea. There is a pool, and the units are lookers —one, two or three bedrooms plus living room, fully equipped kitchen and a minimum of two baths. A good choice for golfing couples and families on extended stays of at least a week. *De luxe.*

The Maui Eldorado Hotel embraces a cluster of low-slung condominium pavilions that contain kitchen-equipped apartments, studio through two bedrooms in size. There are a trio of pools, a grocery store, Kaanapali Beach below, and the Royal Kaanapali Golf Course virtually surrounds the place. Recommended for longish stays, of at least a week, for golfing couples and families. *De luxe*.

The Maui Surf is a handsome S-shaped building—architecturally the most distinguished hotel on the beach—with a perfectly manicured green lawn separating it from beach and sea, and a chaise-encircled pool. Guest rooms are big, tasteful and all with *lanais* (aim for the ocean side), and there are inviting eat-and-drink spots including a great circular main restaurant, coffee shop and bar-lounge-cum-entertainment nightly. Withal, the ambience is a bit bland. Which may, of course, be just what you're looking for. Courteous staff. An Inter-Island hotel. *De luxe*.

The Royal Lahaina is quite the grandest hotel on the Kaanapali scene. And in the best sense of that term, there being much more to it than appears the case as one approaches its nondescript rectangle of a main building. You may or may not go for the corny palm tree murals in many of the bedrooms, but these chambers are otherwise properly luxurious and all have *lanais*. The public areas are a joy: eight swimming pools, putting green, shuffleboard, ten tennis courts, a group of interesting shops, no less than seven drinking parlors and an even eight restaurants, running about as wide a gamut as one could ask (see Chapter 4). Vies with Coco Palms on Kauai as the Queen Bee in the Island Holidays hive. *De luxe*.

The Sheraton-Maui had a great deal going for it as soon as the Sheraton brass determined its site: the splendid Black Rock promontory on Kaanapali Beach, which is not only a ruggedly dramatic spot to look upon, but assures the Sheraton of quite the broadest expanse of beach. The hotel itself is lovely, with its open ceiling, circular garden of a lobby. There are orchid plants at every turn, and the restaurant and bars do not disappoint.

There are a pair of the latter, and of the former (see Chapter 4). Guest rooms are quite the boldest in look of any at Kaanapali, and all are distinguished by moon-shaped *lanais* with green plants overhanging them. And sunset sees the only every-evening torch-lighting ritual at Kaanapali, with after-dark entertainment following. I like. *De luxe.*

Lahaina

The Pioneer Inn is not only plop in the heart of the old whaling town of Lahaina (Chapter 2), it *is* the heart of old Lahaina, and it is to its credit that year in, year out, it remains a casual, informal, nothing-fancy kind of congregating place that just fits the Lahaina personality to a T. Still, unless one has business in Lahaina and is averse to the pleasures of the beach and the golf at next-door Kaanapali or Napili beaches, this is more a place for a drink or a meal or both; its attributes in this area are described in Chapter 4. There are nearly 50 rooms, some in the original building, others in a newer wing, but bear in mind that if the older accommodations are more fun, they are not necessarily more comfortable. *First class.*

Napili Beach

The Napili Kai Beach Club Hotel is the epitome of the casual West Maui resort. The accommodations, in one or another of a conveniently arranged grouping of two-story pavilions, run a gamut in size, but all units have complete kitchens. Still, you may be as lazybones as you like for there's a beachfront restaurant—the Teahouse of the Maui Moon—open for all meals, a bar, and nightly entertainment that is always Hawaiian, and always with microphones *kapu*. The decor throughout is essentially modified Japanese—and nice. There are five pools and a tennis court, and the adjacent Fleming's beach—at which the hotel serves its guests mid-morning coffee—is quite super. The clientele is couples, individuals or families staying an average of a full week. Tour groups are not booked. A special place. *De luxe.*

Napili Shores is set in an elaborately planted garden, with its own beach, a pair of pools, and kitchen-equipped apartments, either studio or one bedroom, and all with *lanais*. A commendable French restaurant (Chapter 4) is on the premises. *De luxe.*

Kihei Area

Hale Pau Hana consists of a pair of beachfront structures containing one-bedroom condominium apartments, all with kitchens. Those in the larger, seven-story building have two baths; those in the smaller, two-story building have one bath each. Functional if not beautiful. Restaurant, bar, pool. *First class.*

Kihei Kai Nana is another condominium apartment complex, with 180 kitchen-equipped one-bedroom apartments. Shopping center next door. Functional if not beautiful. *First class.*

Maui Lu is a good-sized cottage colony with units of varying sizes, all kitchen equipped. Restaurant and bar, two pools, beach across the road. Hardly fancy. *Budget.*

Kula and Haleakala

Kula Lodge is about as atypical Hawaii as you'll find. The elevation is 3,200 feet, and the fireplace in the restaurant is burning even at lunchtime when the sun is shining. The look is appropriately mountain-rustic, with accommodations in five chalets of varying degrees of comfort, detached from the attractive main building wherein are the restaurant, bar and lounge (Chapter 4). A near neighbor is Haleakala, which makes Kula worth considering for lunch enroute, for a big breakfast after having left one's own beach hotel early enough in the morning to see the Haleakala sun rise, or for overnight, in advance of a sun-up drive to Haleakala. *First class.*

Haleakala National Park Cabins: There are only three of them and they are very simple. Each is equipped with water, pit toilet, wood-burning stove for cooking, firewood, candles, cooking and eating utensils, a dozen mattress-and-blanket equipped bunks. You take all the rest, including stout hiking shoes, to gain access. Rates are the equivalent of a couple of cocktails, and you may book by mail; for information: Haleakala National Park, P. O. Box 537, Makawao, Maui, Hawaii 96768. *Budget.*

Hana

The Hana Kai Resort Apartments offer either studio or one-bedroom units—there are 20 all told—with complete kitchens and *lanais* affording views of the water. Nicely situated. *First class.*

The Hotel Hana Maui is a Hawaiian classic. Like a few sister-hotels in the islands—Mauna Kea, the Kahala Hilton, the Royal Hawaiian, Waikea Village—it is one of a kind. The setting—isolated Hana (Chapter 2)—is the primary reason. But the secret of this place's success is the manner in which the hotel complements its environment, refusing concessions to get-with-it, in the manner of more contemporary resorts in less-bucolic settings. At Hana Maui one lives in a garden cottage, either a solitary one, or spacious *lanai*-attached bedrooms that are part of a larger cottage. There is a swimming pool and varied activities—riding, golf, tennis, cycling, even hula or ukelele instruction and other diversion, both daytime and evening (but only, of course, if one wants to do anything other than relax). Plus sublime swimming and sunning at nearby Hamoa Beach. This is a full-American plan resort (there is no place else to eat in the area, even if one wanted to), with bountiful meals, including traditional *luaus* and steak cookouts at the beaches. And nightly Hawaiian entertainment with local folks starring. Remember now: nothing elaborate, except the natural beauty of the setting. Hana Maui is for unwinding. *De luxe*.

SELECTED KAUAI HOTELS

Kalapaki Beach

The Kauai Surf Hotel is the only bona fide skyscraper on Kauai, and there is no gainsaying that it might have blended into the essentially rural environment of this island far more successfully had it been designed with a lower profile. Withal, the Kauai Surf emerges as the ideal all-round resort, there being no major ingredient that it lacks. There is, to start, a magnificent beach at the door—wide white-sands and calm waters that make for fine swimming. There is an 18-hole, par 72 golf course, and adjacent tennis, not to mention the usual aquatic sports, and lessons in *lei* making, ukelele playing and, of course, the hula. Moreover, there are no less than five restaurants (Chapter 4), each distinctive, all of them good. And several places to enjoy a drink, the torchlighting ceremony each sundown, and nightly entertainment. Nicest of all is the spirit of the place: engaging, friendly, smiling, with one of the most thoroughly agreeable staffs of any of the Islands' large hotels. An Inter-Island hotel. *De luxe*.

Wailua Area

Coco Palms is Kauai's, if not all Hawaii's, fairy-tale resort, outrageously corny and yet with the whole bag of tricks so beautifully staged in such a perfectly beautiful setting that you find yourself smitten with the place and wanting to return. Indeed, I suspect none of the major resorts has a bigger or more loyal proportion of regular returnees. Coco Palms became what it is when Mrs. Grace Guslander, wife of Island Holidays' Resorts' Gus Guslander, set her mind to combining some good old-fashioned Hawaiian glamour with the facilities of a de luxe vacation plant. Mrs. Guslander's research into the origins of a plantation of palm trees adjacent to the hotel resulted in legends of the royal Hawaii of old. She then devised what was the Islands' first sunset torch ceremony—often imitated, never equalled. She carried her imagination through to entertainment—all the entertainers at Coco Palms are not only local folks, they are mostly all part of one big happy family. And to decor. Nary a room in Coco Palms has a bathroom washbowl that isn't a giant conch shell. There are several restaurants (one of them recommended in Chapter 5), a variety of watering holes, diverse sports facilities (although, mind, the beach is across the road) and all manner of unexpected treasures, including a Grace Guslander-created Museum-Library of Hawaiiana, and a tiny chapel that has become one of Kauai's most popular wedding locales. The rooms are attractive and run a fairly wide gamut in looks, size and location, not that you can go too far wrong. There are imaginative suites decorated by Mrs. G., too. As previously indicated, the queen bee, along with Maui's Royal Lahaina, of Island Holidays' hive. And great fun even if your name is Ebenezer Scrooge. *De luxe.*

The Islander Inn—a long, rambling and most attractive eight-building complex—is smack in the heart of the Coconut Plantation shopping-restaurant area, with its own beach out back, a pool, and smartly designed, traditional-style bedrooms—all good-sized. Meals are taken in the adjacent Reuben's Restaurant. An Inter-Island hotel. *First class.*

The Kauai Beachboy is a big—250-room—place built around a large pool, with its own beach, a restaurant that operates cafeteria style except at dinner, and a bar. The idea here is economy; either take one of the minimum-rate rooms—which are good buys—or move along to a better category—and better-maintained—hotel. With that proviso: *Budget.*

The Kauai Resort Hotel is a striking-looking place, of modified Polynesian long-house design. Both the main lobby and the restaurant occupy immense high-ceilinged rooms of considerable style. The bedrooms are big and boldly designed; most have *lanais.* And the grounds are lovely, interspersed with rock gardens, cascading waters and carp ponds. Moreover, the food is good—both the buffet lunches and the sit-down dinners. You are likely to run into local residents; the hotel is one of their favorites. A Hawaiian Pacific hotel. *First class.*

Poipu Beach

Kiahuna embraces a group of sloping-roofed, spanking-white structures containing condominium apartments of varying sizes, all with complete kitchens and *lanais,* and all smartly furnished. The beach is out back, and the full-facility Poipu Beach hotels are near-neighbors. *First class.*

The Poipu Beach Hotel is happily casual. All of the 140-plus rooms are kitchenette-equipped and in a melded Japanese-Polynesian decor-blend that works well. There are a restaurant and bar as well, nightly entertainment and an absolutely idyllic beach. An Island Holidays hotel. *First class.*

The Sheraton-Kauai is, to my knowledge, the most intimate Sheraton extant—a casually attractive place, with its 150 rooms and suites—many of them with dramatic cathedral ceilings—housed in a little hamlet of sloped-ceiling pavilions. The main building houses a restaurant whose immense chandeliers are fashioned of local shells. There's a pool to complement the perfectly super beach out back, and there's entertainment nightly in the lounge. An ambience of charm. *De luxe.*

Waiohai may not be all that easy to pronounce, but it's disarmingly casual and friendly enough so that fellow guests, if not the staff, teach you soon enough. This resort consists of a group of cottages of varying sizes, occupying its own secluded acreage directly on the Pacific. The rooms and suites to shoot for are the more distant ones—absolutely dreamy, these—at the ocean's very edge, with the surf just yards away. There's a pool, too, and a simple seaview restaurant, and a terrace for drinks. All in all, a joy. An Island Holidays hotel. *First class.*

Hanalei

Club Méditerranée is rather dramatically perched atop a promontory overlooking the capacious beach at Hanalei Bay (access is via a steepish stairway or an easier-to-manage inclined walk) and embraces a main house-cum-restaurant, a bar/lounge-discothèque-theater building and a cluster of cottages, the lot operated in the get-away-from-it-all style Club Med pioneered in its resorts around the world. The keynote is informality. You book for one-, two- or three-week periods, full American Plan only, spend your days mostly in swimsuits at beach-related activities, and your evenings mostly around the bar, at the disco or at club-sponsored after-dark entertainment. Surfing, sailing, snorkeling, deep-sea fishing and tennis are all free, as regards both equipment and instruction. French-founded and -operated, Club Med happily emphasizes delicious French food (in this case with Hawaiian and Japanese touches), with unlimited house wine at lunch and dinner. Accommodation is mostly in the twin-bedded cottages, but there are rooms in the main house, too; all have private baths. *First class.*

Hanalei Colony Resort is on the beach at Hanalei and offers its guests nearly half a hundred two-bedroom apartments, all with complete kitchens. The Anchorage Restaurant is operated in connection. *First class.*

Princeville Makai Golf Cottages are just the ticket for golfers wanting to take full advantage of the ocean-straddling Princeville golf course—a 27-hole beauty designed by Robert Trent Jones. There are 20 units, mostly all kitchen-equipped; tennis, too. The beach is half a mile distant. *De luxe.*

MOLOKAI HOTELS

The Molokai Hotel is a complex of contemporary Polynesian-style structures on the south shore. The beach is not used, but there is a small pool, a restaurant and bar, and comfortable rooms, all with *lanais. First class.*

Pau Hana Inn includes older as well as more modern accommodations; I would counsel only the latter. There is an atmospheric banyan court for drinks and dancing, a pleasant restaurant, and a friendly bar which, like the restaurant, is popular with Molokai residents. *Budget.*

LANAI'S HOTEL

Lanai Lodge, the island's sole hostelry, is frequented by the locals, and by residents of the bigger islands, anxious for a simple, restful day or two. The setting is a pine-forested bluff above little Lanai City. There are just under a dozen rooms, all with private bath, and an unpretentious restaurant-bar. Remember now: it's not fancy. *Budget.*

4

Hawaii to Eat and Drink

SETTING THE CULINARY SCENE

If it is true that one eats extraordinarily well only rarely in Hawaii, it follows, too, that the positively unsatisfactory dining experience is even rarer to behold. The point I mean to make is that Hawaii, as the great American resort, gives its customers pretty much what they want. (The big exception in this regard is that it does some supersalesmanship in convincing them to experience at least one *luau*—the high-profit mass-tourism variation on the theme of traditional Hawaiian feasting.) Hawaiian restaurant cooking, at least for the great visitor market, is pretty much meat-and-potatoes, and no nonsense. (If the visitor invariably sees rice on menus as an alternative to potatoes—which he does outside of the tourist hotels—this is a concession to the Oriental-influenced local diet; residents, regardless of ethnic identification, are big rice eaters.) There are other foods that are popular with locals regardless of background and that reflect Hawaii's melting-pot heritage: *saimin,* a Japanese-origin noodle dish flavored with a sauce usually made of meat and vegetables and sold at fast-food outlets statewide; *sushi,* also Japanese, and consisting of seasoned rice, with a seaweed or bean-curd covering; *sashimi,* fresh raw fish—tuna, usually in Hawaii—dipped in a hot sauce; meats (including hamburgers) served *teriyaki* style, which means, essentially, a ginger-marinade seasoning; *Portuguese sausages*—a contribution of the Portuguese community originally from Madeira and the Azores; and *Hawaiian* foods including *poi,* the Hawaiian staple in the manner of potatoes or rice, and made from the root of the taro plant, roast pig and *lomi-lomi* salmon (standard fare at the commercial *luaus* as described in Chapter 5). Along with steaks, prime ribs of beef and hamburgers, seafood plays a major dietary role, much of it centering on local catches, especially—and happily—the tasty fish called *mahi-mahi*. There are a number of Japanese restaurants. They are invariably good—and much better than the Chinese restaurants, which tend to be great disappointments to Mainlanders who know the superb Chinese cuisine of major cities from San Francisco to New York. European specialty restaurants are harder to come upon, although there is, *merci le bon Dieu,* some stellar French representation, and some Italian, although considerably less of the latter than is usually the proportion in Mainland cities. Desserts tend to be delicious—often employing local ingredients like pineapple, passionfruit, macadamia nuts, papaya and coconut as flavorings. Bread and rolls are a distinct disappointment, for the most part. Lightish lunches—hamburgers, club sandwiches, chef and fruit salads—are the rule, and are generally appetizing. Breakfasts are often served buffet style, although many places considerately give one the choice of ordering made-to-order morning meals, a chief advantage of which is that one's eggs will be custom-made. It is in this area that the bountiful breakfast buffets often disappoint; often one's only egg choice is from a pan of several dozen that have been scrambled hours before and are being kept warm over a steam table. Snacking is a round-the-clock habit, from the beaches to the boulevards. The time-honored habit in bars and cocktail lounges—the offering of the delicious complimentary hot canapés that in Hawaii are called *puu puus*—is almost extinct. Now one is lucky to settle for peanuts with a drink. There is not a bar in the state that I know of that would offer the exorbitantly priced, locally cultivated macadamias.

Meal prices run a wide gamut, although most places are moderately priced and many inexpensive. As on the Mainland, the very top bracket restaurants are costly and, for the most part, deserve to be; the better among them end up being good value.

In no major resort area of the planet, save Acapulco, is dress more casual. In all of Honolulu, not more than half a handful of places ask men to wear jackets, and even where this is the rule, neckties are optional. Women, in the better places, tend to put their new long *muumuus* to good use. The result is that everyone looks good and feels comfortable.

Not unsurprisingly, dining options are at their greatest on Oahu. On the Neighbor Islands, one is pretty much limited to the hotels and the independent restaurants of the towns, all of which are small in contrast to cosmopolitan Honolulu. Even so, the Neighbor Islands visitor is not without variety, and does well to sample the restaurants of places other than his hotel.

What follows are a *selective* recommendation of places to eat, island by island. By and large, they are spots that I enjoy, for one reason or another. It is important to note that service in Hawaii, as everywhere in the world, is a sometime thing, and that the restaurant where I have been so satisfied can be a distinct disappointment to you. Not only service staffs change; chefs do, too. And with their comings and goings, quality of food can vary. So, of course, can maintenance. These factors borne in mind, I am confident that what follows will serve as an Inner Man guide during the course of a Hawaiian holiday. Please note my price groups: *Expensive, Moderate, Budget.*

SELECTED OAHU RESTAURANTS

The quantity of restaurants on Oahu is staggering. What I have done is break down my recommendations into a dozen categories presented alphabetically, beginning with admirable breakfast locales. Restaurants within each category are reviewed in alphabetical order, too.

Breakfasting in Waikiki

It's fun to leave your own hotel and move around for breakfast; there's no nicer time for a Waikiki walk than early morning, and the cost factor enters in, too. Breakfast is an ideal way for the budget traveler to sample the food, surroundings and service of the better hotels, where other meals might cost more than he would want to spend.

The often-encountered buffets are invariably good buys in that they are organized on an all-you-can-eat basis; eat late enough and you can skip lunch, or settle for a pick-me-up on the beach.

Hanohano Room, Sheraton-Waikiki Hotel: An exterior elevator—glass-walled so you get the view as you ascend—takes you to the top of the Sheraton-Waikiki tower, affording you the opportunity for a meal that would cost considerably more at dinner, which is what this elaborate room was designed for. The panoramic views—from Diamond Head to Pearl Harbor—are gorgeous. *Moderate.*

Princess Kaiulani Hotel: Take your choice here, waitress service in the cheery Café Colonnade, or perhaps more fun, a bountiful buffet served at umbrella tables flanking the swimming pool. *Moderate.*

The Rigger (Kalakaua Avenue): The club breakfasts are good buys, tasty, and courteously presented. *Budget.*

Smorgy's (Coral Sea Hotel, Reef Hotel, Outrigger Hotel): The queue—and there is invariably a queue—moves faster than you might think. The draw is the best buffet-breakfast buy in town. Choose either the Reef or Outrigger hotel locations, and you have the added bonus of an alfresco seaside setting. *Budget.*

The Snack Shop (Kalakaua Avenue, Diamond Head of the main entrance of the Royal Hawaiian Hotel) is never without its fair share of customers, even early morning. But the lines are worth the wait. Club or à la carte breakfasts are tasty and good buys, with the baked goods a highlight. *Budget.*

The Surfrider Hotel: The big, bright Niumalu Coffee Shop serves up a super buffet, but you may order from the menu, too. Lovely service, and with tables set outside on the oceanfront *lanai,* as well as indoors. *Moderate.*

Surf Room, Royal Hawaiian Hotel: Getting there is half the fun of an early morning walk through the gardens and lobby of the Royal to reach this casual, semi-outdoors, oceanfront restaurant. As for viands, the fare centers around an especially nice buffet, but you may order from a menu, too. A classic Waikiki dining spot. *Moderate.*

Chinese

The Lotus Moon (Princess Kaiulani Hotel) offers about as much variety in its menu as one can find in Hawaii, where Chinese pretty much means run-of-the-mill Cantonese. Peking Duck is a delicious specialty, the decor is appropriately Chinese, and the staff likewise. *Moderate.*

Patti's Chinese Kitchen (Ala Moana Shopping Center) is an absolutely fabulous Chinese cafeteria. If the fare is not Mandarin, it is bountiful, copious and in astonishing variety. The big seller is beef brocoli—all Hawaii's favorite Chinese dish—but you find egg rolls, duck in infinite variations, spareribs, pork dishes galore, Chinese mushrooms in many styles, and a favorite with locals at lunchtime—combination plates. *Budget.*

Winter Garden (Kahala Mall Shopping Center): Honolulans like this one, with the range of regional cuisines about the most extensive in town, even including some spicy Szechuan dishes. The big specialty, believe it or not, is a remarkable candied apple dish that you simply have to try. *Moderate.*

Wo Fat (115 North Hotel Street, downtown): The Chinatown setting is as significant as the food—a turn-of-century building, two very grand stories, with a little pagoda topping off the whole. The main dining room is up one flight—high-ceilinged, capacious, straight out of a slinky old B-movie. Lots of local businessmen are among the lunchers. The fare is competent albeit unexciting Cantonese; the crispy duck is a very good bet. *Moderate.*

Delicatessen

Lyn's Delicatessen (Ala Moana Shopping Center): The real thing —hot corned beef, pastrami, salami, dill pickles, cole slaw, potato salad. Just the kind of nostalgic pick-me-up you may require at mid-point—or, for that matter, at *any* point—in your holiday. *Moderate.*

French

Chez Michel (2126-B Kalakaua Avenue) is located toward the rear of an unprepossessing Waikiki commercial building. But you must not let the look of the place deter you. Within, the ambience is delightful, the service admirable and, most important, the food first-rate. There are daily lunch specials—boeuf Bourguignon, tournedos sauce Béarnaise, for example. As well as non-Gallic sandwiches and salads. Dinner is much more gastronomically interesting, with regulars including the house's own onion soup and terrine, as well as such entrées as frog's legs, veal sautéed *grand-mère* style, roast duck and roast lamb. The vegetables are fresh, salads are served with the house *vinaigrette,* and desserts run to cherries jubilee, fresh pineapple with kirsch, strawberries Romanoff and mangoes in champagne. Good wine list, too. Depending upon how much you eat and drink and whether it's lunch (*moderate*) or a more elaborate dinner, *moderate to expensive.*

Michel's (Colony Surf Hotel) is unadulterated French, and in the grand manner, the kind of place where you want to read the menu over carefully, not missing out on the possibility of any of the authentically prepared dishes. The dinner hour is busy and smart and dressy; this is one of the very few places in the state that ask men to wear jackets. The staff is professional—no smiling albeit uninformed kids taking orders here—and the fare delicious. You might start off with *escargots* or *vichyssoise* or the imported *foie gras* from Strasbourg. Entrée specialties include veal *Cordon Bleu,* or the *châteaubriand* steak for two. The fresh vegetables are exceptional. Salads are, too. Desserts are honored by a separate menu card of their own. Select the Coconut Kona Sundae, a pastry, the simple *crème caramel* or the rich chocolate mousse. There are flaming sweets, too—bananas, cherries or *crêpes.* And a creditable cheese platter—among the few in Hawaii. Or finish off with a rich coffee concoction (*diablo* or *capuchino*) in lieu of dessert. Michel's selection of liqueurs and cognacs is among the most extensive in the islands, and this place's Sunday brunch—I recommend the *crêpes* or the omelettes—is at once delicious and moderately tabbed. Otherwise: *cher, très cher.*

Gala and Gorgeous

The Maile Restaurant (Kahala Hilton Hotel) takes its name from a species of plant whose leaves the old Hawaiian *alii* employed for state ceremonies and are still fashioned into *leis* for very special occasions. That is what the Maile is for: very special occasions. Happily, it is not big. The chefs are able to cook with care, and the staff is able to take a personal interest in each party. The setting—you reach the room after descending from the lobby via a winding staircase framed by orchids and lava rock—is one of flowers, green plants and cascading water. The menu card, an enormous orange and silver affair, runs a tempting gamut. Start with the Mahimami Caprice—the fresh local fish fried in butter, served on creamed mushrooms and glazed. Continue with chilled gazpacho or lobster bisque. Choose from such entrées as beef Stroganoff, prime New York steak *au poivre,* or a *kumu*—one of the tastier island fish—baked whole, with fennel and Pernod. There are favorites like prime ribs of beef, and thick sirloins, and the desserts are sumptuous, including a memorable soufflé Grand Marnier and macadamia nut cream pie. Elegant. Delicious. And dressy, which means jackets, gentlemen, please. *Expensive.*

Michel's (Colony Surf Hotel): See French restaurants above.

Monarch Room (Royal Hawaiian Hotel): This is traditional Waikiki at its most posh. Dinner and the show at the Monarch Room is as essential to a Hawaii holiday as watching a Waikiki sunset or photographing the dancers at the Kodak Hula Show. The setting is a great chandeliered salon, rich with reds and golds dominating the decor, and a dressy clientele. (Men will want to wear jackets here.) The menu, as is generally the case where entertainment is a major part of the scene, is more limited than in many restaurants, with substantial stand-bys like broiled sirloin and filet mignon the favored entrées. *Expensive.*

The Summit (Ala Moana Hotel) is at its most stylish at dinner time, when the view from on high—the setting is the thirty-sixth floor, and there is no higher-up restaurant in town—is of a blinking, twinkling Honolulu—illuminated ships at sea, the Waikiki hotels outlined by their lights and the silhouette of downtown. Which is not to say that the vistas take precedence over the food. Summit meals—blue points on the half shell, spinach salad prepared at table with a hot dressing, rack of lamb, Puget Sound salmon—are memorable. And the management prides itself on an extensive, high-quality wine list. Lunch is less costly and less elaborate with the advantage of the same view, daytime variation. And Sunday brunch is a very good and tasty buy. At dinner: *expensive.*

The Third Floor (Hawaiian Regent Hotel) is the most imaginatively conceived and decorated of Honolulu restaurants—an unlikely but extraordinarily successful meld of waterfalls, open-beam ceilings, towering plants, koa-wood wall mosaics, mouth-watering still-lifes of fruits and fishes and other edibles, and high-back rattan chairs surrounding tables beneath an array of multi-colored banners, King Arthur style. All this with equally imaginative—and delicious—edibles, and an exceptional choice of wines. Appetizers include papaya with prosciutto, or *sashimi*. Main dishes run to saddle of venison, roast pheasant, thick-cut sirloins, or French-style *châteaubriand*. The vegetables are all fresh. Desserts are superb, especially the cakes and pastries, wheeled over on a cart. Itinerant minstrels serenade each table as they make their rounds, service is skilled and smiling, and the crowds—men wear jackets—is as attractive as the room is festive. *Expensive.*

The Top of the I (Ilikai Hotel) is for good viewing and good eating. The spectacular panorama is of Waikiki, the mountains, the sea and downtown from the nether reaches of the skyscraping Ilikai. It is memorable enough at lunch, when the menu is moderate-priced and concentrates on sandwiches and salads. But it is positively romantic at dinner, with candlelight, and—worth noting —a well-priced table d'hôte meal with five entrées, as well as an elaborate à la carte, with such specialties as *tournedos Périgourdine* and stuffed trout with crabmeat, following starters like oysters Rockefeller or onion soup, and with desserts that include a rich and lovely pear *Belle Hélène* and Hawaiian bananas converted into a cream pie. Service is smooth and there is entertainment and music for dinner dancing. *Expensive.*

Good Buys

The Captain's Galley (Diamond Head Wing, Moana Hotel) has the combined advantage of oceanfront setting (with some of the tables on the *lanai*), a solid-value table d'hôte menu usually including both steak and seafood. Dinner—by candlelight—only. *Moderate.*

Cock's Roost (International Market Place): This one, over the Colonial House Cafeteria (see below), offers broiled favorites—steaks, seafood, beef, chicken—most reasonably and in a pleasant setting. *Budget.*

Colonial House Cafeteria (International Market Place) is a long-time stand-by, for cheap, appetizing breakfasts, lunches and dinners. *Budget.*

Kuhio Torch Restaurant (Kuhio Hotel, 2345 Kuhio Avenue): Upstairs, on the attractive pool deck, and offering a tasty bargain-priced buffet dinner usually including roast beef among the three entrées. *Budget.*

Liberty House Garden Restaurant (Ala Moana Shopping Center): The Liberty House department store at Ala Moana is by far its most attractive outlet, and this upstairs restaurant is in keeping. It's a beauty, and with value-packed table d'hôte meals. *Budget–Moderate.*

Prince Kuhio's Restaurant (Ala Moana Shopping Center) is at once a looker, in the ornate style of the monarchy at turn-of-century, and with exceptionally well-priced table d'hôte lunches and dinners embracing steaks, seafood and even a Hawaiian platter. Agreeable service, too. *Moderate.*

Sheraton-Waikiki Hotel Ocean Terrace Coffee Shop: The lure in this gay and casually got-up room is the buffet dinner, with a surprisingly wide choice and modest tabs. *Budget.*

Smorgy's (Reef Hotel, Outrigger Hotel, Coral Seas Hotel): This trio of bargain-spot cafeterias is hardly a secret. It has countless devotees. Breakfast is earlier recommended. Lunches and dinners are also rather astonishing buys when you consider that this is a help-yourself proposition and that there are some forty different types of foods from which to choose. You may not like them all, but you're bound to find enough to please. *Budget*.

Snack Shop (Diamond Head of Royal Hawaiian Hotel, Kalakaua Avenue): A coffee shop with a Southern California kind of life style. The usual fare for such places, invariably well prepared, with wickedly luscious pies—banana cream, macadamia nut, lemon meringue, boysenberry—the specialties. *Budget*.

Surfrider Hotel Niumalu Coffee Shop: Not to be outdone by its down-the-avenue counterpart at the Sheraton-Waikiki, this good-looking place—one of the biggest such on the beach—offers a super buffet dinner, too. I have earlier recommended it for breakfast, and it is also pleasant at lunch. Tables outdoors on the *lanai,* if you like. *Budget*.

Woolworth's (Kalakaua Avenue in the heart of Waikiki, and Ala Moana Shopping Center): At both big Woolworth's, eating is convenient and value-packed. In each location there is a spacious waitress-service restaurant—with substantial entrées including steaks on the table d'hôte lunch and dinner menus; and there are snack counters for on-the-run orders, as well. *Budget*.

Italian

Trattoria (in the Edgewater Hotel, 2168 Kalia Road) is the genuine article, which means Mediterranean decor, mostly Italian serving staff, not to mention a chef from the Peninsula, who specializes in northern Italian dishes—delicious variations on a theme of veal, superb pastas with a variety of sauces and quite as *al dente* as you want them; good *espresso,* and appropriate Italian wines. The only local ingredient is the live music, which you can't fault. Book in advance and be prepared for a wait over drinks in the bar. *Moderate–Expensive*.

Japanese

Furusato (Second floor, Waikiki Grand Hotel, 134 Kapahulu Avenue, just off Kalakaua) is about as authentic a Japanese restaurant as you'll find in a town full of authentic—and first-rate—Japanese restaurants. Don't let the location—a second-rate hotel—put you off. The restaurant is independent, simply renting the space. The moment you enter, you are in Nippon. The place is invariably jammed (with the overwhelming majority of customers Japanese tourists), the anxious-to-please kimono-clad waitresses are dashing furiously about, and the food is the genuine article—and delicious. Dinners are complete, with the interesting specialty a steak—Genghis Khan by name—made on the hibachi at one's table. *Yakitori* (broiled chicken on bamboo skewers), and *tempura* (deep-fried shrimp, fish and assorted vegetables) are excellent here. There is a special *sukiyaki* dinner, too. *Moderate*.

Momoyama (Princess Kaiulani Hotel) offers the Japanese regulars, as well as such specialties as *yaki-niku,* a beef dish prepared at table. Don't let the setting—an occidental-style Sheraton hotel—convey the impression that this is not the real thing. Chefs, waitresses, captains—all are Japanese. So is the decor. And so are many of the clientele. *Moderate*.

Miyako (Ala Moana Shopping Center) is a mass-production Japanese place in the heart of Ala Moana. The specialty is take-out orders for workers in the neighborhood. But there are bargain-price plate lunches, with such main courses as pork *teriyaki* and shrimp *tempura*. And if you're hungry for a snack, why not a *teriyaki* hot dog? *Budget*.

Mon Cher Ton Ton (Ala Moana Hotel) takes its French name from a decidedly Japanese restaurant in the Japanese capital. The diminutive for "my dear uncle," in French, is the name of a popular Tokyo eatery. Ala Moana's is popular, too; quite the smartest looking of the Japanese spots in Honolulu, with a tempting menu whose highlights include *yaki tori,* lobster *teriyaki,* shrimp *kushi-yaki,* and *sukiyaki,* which is delicious here. The waitresses are Japanese dolls, and there is a section of Teppan tables where chefs prepare steak and seafood dishes right before you. Lunch and dinner, both table d'hôte and à la carte. *Moderate.*

Polynesian

Kon Tiki (Sheraton-Waikiki Hotel) is an amusing put-on. Getting there is all a part of the show, and includes an elevator ride from the little entranceway: up you go in a hydraulic bamboo bungalow. The room itself is a modishly embellished grass shack where you may order just about anything you like, including so-called Polynesian dishes (these somehow or other include Indian curries), as well as more prosaic things like steak, chicken and broiled *mahi-mahi. Moderate.*

The Tahitian Lanai (Waikikian Hotel) is the principal restaurant of a hotel whose entire look is Polynesian. This one is a charmer, alongside the hotel pool, which in turn is alongside an honest-to-goodness lagoon. You may order Polynesian specialties as well as occidental stand-bys like steak or prime ribs. Whatever, the ambience is a delight. *Moderate.*

Trader Vic's (International Market Place) was approached by at least one sampler with skepticism. Could a restaurant in as tourist-trod a setting as the market place be first-rate? The answer is a strong affirmative. The decor is what Trader Vic made famous when he pioneered these Polynesian shenanigans, and its amusing. The food runs to barbecued spareribs, pressed almond duck, fried jumbo shrimps, steak *teriyaki,* crab *foo yong.* There are curries and Hawaiian dishes, too, and the banana fritters are a super dessert. Reasonably priced complete lunches, too (with the hot *puu-puu* platter a delicious choice). *Moderate.*

Seafood

Fisherman's Wharf (Kewalo Basin) is here included only because you may have heard of it because of its location. Well, the setting—overlooking the Kewalo Basin and its vessels—is atmospheric enough. But the food, to be polite about it, is pedestrian. Lunch or dinner. *Budget–Moderate*.

The Ship's Tavern (Surfrider Hotel) is a sea-view spot with a nautical look about it, a jaunty atmosphere and some tasty specialties, most definitely including the clam chowder served in a jumbo tureen. You pick your lobsters from a tank, and the crab-stuffed flounder is delicious. Meat dishes for landlubbers. Dinner only. *Moderate*.

The Voyager Fish Grotto (Travelodge, 1850 Ala Moana Boulevard) is reached from the cramped and unattractive lobby of this hotel, and is therefore more agreeable than one might imagine, with a dark-beamed pubby look. The menu is mainly marine—seafood curry, lobster thermidor, Pacific oysters, broiled fish-of-the-day; steaks, too, if you insist. *Moderate*.

Steaks and Roast Beef

Buzz's (Reef Lanai Hotel, Saratoga Avenue, near Kalia Road) is unpretentious albeit inviting, with reasonably priced broiled specialties including steak and *mahi-mahi*. Casual. *Budget–Moderate*.

Byron II Steak House (Ala Moana Shopping Center) is handsome, nicely staffed and with delicious full-course sirloin-steak dinners its specialty. Special lunches, too, at which the omelettes are a good bet. *Moderate*.

Canlis (2100 Kalakaua Avenue) is here included because it is an old Waikiki stand-by and because its West Coast branches are well known to many visitors. I have been visiting the Waikiki Canlis—with much pleasure—over a period of years, but my most recent dinner was a distinct disappointment. Service was gruff and unsmiling. My party waited almost an hour for a table, with an advance reservation, but not a hint of an apology was given for this excessive delay, and the treatment at the table was even less genial, if possible. The food was edible, no more. Canlis—still a nice looking place—has apparently let success go to its head, at least in Honolulu. A pity. *Expensive.*

Chuck's Cellar (Reef Towers and Outrigger East hotels) specializes in prime ribs of beef, and does so very well indeed. You help yourself to salad from a counter, and to French bread, as well. Steaks, too. Good value. *Moderate.*

Mike's (Beach Walk, *makai* of Kalakaua Avenue) is a broil-your-own place, and that includes chickens as well. You help yourself to all the salad you want. *Budget.*

Reuben's (Kahala Mall) specializes in steaks and other broiled dishes. The setting is festive, the service generally genial, and there is entertainment at dinner. An island-wide chain. *Moderate.*

The Safari Steakhouse (Sheraton-Waikiki Hotel) is all browns and blacks and whites with chrome accents and African photo-murals embellishing the walls—very smart to look upon. The fare is beef—steaks and ribs. And some seafood, too. *Moderate–Expensive.*

Whaler's Broiler (Ala Moana Hotel) evokes mid-nineteenth-century Hawaii, when the port of Lahaina was the pre-eminent whaling port of the planet. You may begin with Whaler's Grog (ask for the recipe) and go on to prime ribs carved from a wagon rolled to your table. Or try a steak dish; the beef tenderloin is tasty. Hearty soups and desserts, too. The waiters are got-up as sailors of yore. Lunch and dinner-cum-entertainment. *Moderate.*

Very Special

The Banyan Court (Moana Hotel) for long one of the most beloved of Waikiki congregating points, is now occupied evenings with a noisy Polynesian-style revue, so that just about the only time you can have a peaceful meal at this lovely spot in this historic hotel—Waikiki's oldest, dating to 1901—is Saturday noon, when the "Hawaii Calls" radio show is broadcast from there. The service is buffet, and I suggest you book in advance. *Moderate.*

The Continental Cafeteria (Ala Moana Shopping Center) could happen only in Honolulu. What makes it special is its quartet of separate serving sections, reflecting the ethnic composition of the state. There's a section each for "American," Chinese, Japanese and Hawaiian foods, with the latter as good a spot as any to become acquainted with such local dishes as *lomi-lomi* salmon, *poi,* smoked-pig *luau* style, and the local fish, *mahi-mahi,* prepared Hawaiian fashion. *Budget.*

Farrell's Ice Cream Parlor (International Market Place) is among the relatively few ice cream spots in Waikiki, surprising in a tourist-packed tropical resort. Take your choice of sodas, sundaes, shakes, malts, cones. It's all delicious and the place has a gay, old-fashioned look. Open late. *Budget.*

Honolulu Academy of Arts Garden Café (900 South Beretania Street): The Establishment ladies, whose province this first-rate museum has long been (Chapter 2) volunteer to operate this semi-alfresco restaurant, to raise money for the museum. The menu is limited to a different set-lunch each day—invariably distinctive and delicious. It could, for example, comprise asparagus soup, a turkey sandwich with freshly made mayonnaise on home-style whole-wheat bread, a salad—fresh fruit or an unusual one melding fresh peas, celery, ham and water chestnuts— a do-it-yourself sundae with a choice of scrumptious cakes for dessert; plus iced tea with fresh mint or coffee. No bar. Lunch only, Tuesday through Friday, noon to 1:30 P.M., and you are advised to book in advance. *Budget.*

The Rose & Crown (King's Alley Shopping Center) is a genuine English pub—serving Watney's Red Barrel—in the core of Waikiki. Go for drinks, lunch or dinner; specialties include steak and mushroom pie. Quiche Lorraine and sandwiches, too. And English drinks like Black and Tan, Shandy and hard cider. *Budget.*

Smitty's Pancake House (Ala Moana Shopping Center) is not all that different from your run-of-the-mill pancake house at home, except that it has specialty pancakes with Hawaiian fillings; most especially the pineapple ones. *Budget.*

Waioli Tea Room (3016 Oahu Avenue, Moana Valley) occupies a bucolic bit of acreage out in the country. It's a perfect lunch spot. Take a look at the little house in which Robert Louis Stevenson stayed during his visit in the nineties, wander through the grounds, and have one of the set-lunches—which might feature fried chicken of boiled *mahi-mahi*. Please sample the home-baked cakes and pastries, which are also sold from a take-out counter; I heartily counsel the pineapple brownies. The operators are none other than our friends the Salvation Army, on the scene a long time in Oahu; I first knew them during World War II when they ran a beach canteen for service personnel. *Budget.*

The Willows (901 Hausten Street, in a quiet Honolulu residential district) occupies a clutch of spacious pavilions overlooking a king-size carp pond. The same family has operated it since its

opening during World War II. You lunch or dine either in one of
the pavilions or alfresco, under umbrellas. (The setting is lovely.)
Drinks are good, and the fare ranges from club sandwiches, a
chicken curry or a seafood salad at lunch, to more substantial
dishes—roast turkey, broiled spring rack of lamb, a steak-and-
lobster platter—at dinner. Desserts, especially the sky-high pies,
are sumptuous, and the service is what you might call Down
Home Hawaiian. Very nice indeedy. Best to book. *Moderate.*

SELECTED BIG ISLAND RESTAURANTS

Kailua-Kona

Chuck's Steak House (Alii Road, Kailua-Kona) is much simpler
in appearance than its counterparts on Maui and Oahu, but it is a
reliable spot for steaks and other broiled specialties, at dinner.
Moderate.

Ed & Don's (Marlin Plaza, Alii Road, Kailua-Kona) is a branch
of an island-wide ice cream chain, but the point to note here, aside
from the frozen sweets, is cheap doughnut-and-coffee breakfasts.
Budget.

Hotel King Kamehameha-Hotel Kona makes a specialty of seafood. Kona Coast fresh fish as well as imported lobsters and the
like. *Moderate–Expensive.*

Kona Galley (Alii Road, Kailua-Kona) occupies the upper deck
of a two-story, heart-of-town structure. The view of the bay is
pleasant and so is the food, with fresh Kona Coast fish especially
good. Complete lunches, dinners. *Moderate.*

Kona Hilton Hotel: There are several possibilities here, all commendable. The Hele Mai Dining Room is a bay-front restaurant,
with lovely views. There is a roast beefery, the Kona Rib Hale,

which prides itself on the best beef on the coast, and there is, as well, the more recent Pasta Korner—with an Italian chef preparing his specialties. Coffee shop, too. *Moderate–Expensive.*

Kona Pasta House (Alii Road, Kailua-Kona) occupies the upstairs pavilion of a mid-village building, affording a view of the bay, and with both pizza and pasta on the menu. *Moderate.*

Kona Tei (Alii Road, Kailua-Kona) is an attractive upstairs place in the shopping center opposite the main harbor. Japanese food, with Teppan—cooked at table—dishes the pride of the house. *Moderate.*

The Marlin Hut (Marlin Plaza Shopping Center, Kailua-Kona) is a smallish, unpretentious place serving breakfast, lunch and dinner, with an alfresco section, and a loyal local clientele. Stews and hamburgers are among the house dishes. *Budget.*

The Pottery (Main Highway just outside of Kailua-Kona) is at once a pottery and a restaurant. You eat on crockery that may have only recently emerged from the kiln, as you watch more being made, while you dine. Try the steak-and-scampi platter, or the Cornish hen. *Moderate.*

Reuben's (Alii Road, Kailua-Kona) is oceanfront, handsome, and with the same tasty broiled specialties—mainly steaks—that you know from its other outposts. Recommended for breakfast, too: take a *lanai* table and order the pancake sandwich. *Moderate.*

Hilo

Dragon Inn (172 Kilauea Avenue) is a cleaner-than-clean downtown spot, with an absolutely enormous Hilo-grown orchid plant gracing each table. The fare can be interesting Cantonese, especially if you skip the prosaic combination plates. The chicken with

Chinese mushrooms, is hardly to be despised. *Budget* if you order a combination plate; otherwise *moderate*.

Crescent Manor (139 Kapiolani Street) is an upstairs place with an agreeable, albeit fairly standard, menu and views of town and harbor. *Moderate*.

Hibachi (107 Banyan Drive) is of-this-moment Japanese, with a nice garden and futuristic decor. *Moderate*.

Ken's House of Pancakes (1730 Kamehameha Avenue) is at once a coffee shop and a cocktail lounge. Both are attractive. The former serves appetizing breakfasts, lunches and dinners; worth noting: this never closes. *Budget*.

The Orchid Room (Orchid Isle Hotel) is a well-proportioned well-operated tropically decorated restaurant that serves breakfast, lunch and dinner, with the last-mentioned the most festive and fun of the lot, thanks to soft lights, an interesting menu (Italian dishes like veal scallopine and chicken cacciatore, along with steak and local seafood) and live entertainment. *Moderate— Expensive*.

The Voyager Restaurant (Travelodge, 121 Banyan Drive) is an attractive room, with fairly standard dishes—steaks, broiled *mahi-mahi* and the like—which it prepares well and serves nicely. *Moderate*.

The Kupuna Room (Waiakea Resort Village): If you have an opportunity for but one dressy dinner during your stay in Hilo, this should be where you have it. The setting is spectacular and the fare and presentation match it. House specials run to seafood, a Hawaiian variation on the theme of France's bouillabaisse, sautéed scampi, fillet of turbot in a wine sauce, and *mahi-mahi* as you haven't had it before—cooked in parchment and combined with crabmeat, shrimps and mushrooms. There are beef dishes, too; the filet mignon with Béarnaise sauce is masterful. And the salads are lovely. So is that Waiakea Village service, and the live entertainment. *Expensive.*

Woolworth's (Haiki and Keawe streets) has a good-sized restaurant and fountain with complete lunches and dinner. Additionally, there's a snack bar in the rear of the store. *Budget.*

Kamuela

Mauna Kea Beach Hotel: It is not likely that you will be in the neighborhood of Mauna Kea Beach Hotel at dinnertime unless you're staying there. But if you are, head for one of the hotel restaurants to get an idea of how Rockresorts understate elegance. The menus are mostly American-Continental, with some local specialties. Meats are top grade. The fish is today's, vegetables likewise, and pastries and breads are a Mauna Kea specialty. (When you help yourself to the banana bread, think of me.) What is more likely than your being around at dinnertime is that you will pass through at midday. By all means, make it for lunch. The buffet on the outdoor terrace, overlooking the beach and the Pacific, is a Big Island institution. Indeed, it is a Rockresort institution, as you might recall from the chain's hotels in Puerto Rico and the Virgin Islands. For lunch, *moderate.* For dinner, *expensive.*

SELECTED MAUI RESTAURANTS

Kahului

The Aloha Restaurant is a simple enough proposition—cinderblock walls, linoleum floor and the like. But it is spotless, inviting and, what's more, the only place on Maui where Hawaiian dishes

are a specialty. If roast pig, *lomi-lomi* salmon, *poi* and the like are
your bag—or if you reach Maui without having tried them—this
is worthy of a lunch or dinner stop. *Budget.*

The Landing is a big, good-looker of a place, with a nicely varied
menu—steaks, seafood, salads, with the added filip of an adjacent
antique railroad car now seeing service as a bar. *Moderate.*

Kaanapali Beach

The Chart House occupies cosy quarters over a store, at the edge
of Kaanapali. The specialty is steaks; and are they ever delicious.
Moderate.

Chuck's Steak House (Whalers Village Shopping Center) is a
smart double-level restaurant, whose New York sirloins are, in at
least one taster's view, unsurpassed in Hawaii. They're served
with baked potato or French fries, and salad from a help-yourself bar. Live music emanates from the bar area. *Moderate.*

Moby Dick's (in a detached building on the grounds of the Royal
Lahaina Hotel) may well be the best seafood house in the state.
Nowhere is the menu more seriously maritime, with the fare
ranging from *coquilles St. Jacques* through poached fillet of sole
and eastern scallops *Provençale* to Alaska king crab and broiled
Australian rock lobster. This place has a reputation, so booking
in advance is absolutely essential. *Expensive.*

Don the Beachcomber (Royal Lahaina Hotel): The Maui outpost of the ubiquitous Mr. Don. You will recognize the South Seas
hodgepodge decor and the menu which, happily, is more Chinese
than anything else. Book in advance. *Moderate–Expensive.*

Royal Kaanapali Golf Course 19th Hole: A simple terrace turned
into a simple spot for a sandwich lunch; cold ones, hamburgers or

hot Reubens. The ace in the hole is the super view of the hotels, the beach and sea below. *Budget.*

Sheraton-Maui Hotel Black Rock Terrace: Happiness is lunch of a fine day at this open-to-the-beach restaurant, where the specialty is a sumptuous buffet, with both hot and cold dishes. Have a chef's salad, instead, or even a pastrami on rye. The same restaurant—candlelit—becomes very smart at dinner, especially if there's a full moon. *Moderate* at lunch. *Moderate–Expensive* at dinner.

Napili Beach

Pineapple Hill occupies a rather grand, one-time mansion, high on a hill and with a sublime view of the sea. The gustatory lures are local turtle steak, if you please, or somewhat more prosaic, roast duck. The trick is to arrive just before sunset so that you can be sipping your cocktail while the sun is setting over the islands of Molokai and Lanai on the horizon. Dinner only. *Expensive.*

Le Tournedos (Napili Shores Hotel) is Frenchy-French-from-France—the genuine article. The room is an attractive one and the menu is essentially an extensive series of variations on the theme of the French steaks known as *tournedos*. They are served a dozen ways, but there are other dishes, of fish and poultry, not to mention starters like snails and onion soup. *Moderate–Expensive.*

Lahaina

Banyan Inn serves dinner—mostly local Maui beef appearing as tasty steaks—in its capacious garden. Other entrées, too, and homemade pies (good) for dessert. An especially interesting wine list. *Moderate.*

The Lahaina Broiler is central, attractive, and a long-time congregating place, for breakfast, lunch and dinner, with an over-the-water situation. *Moderate.*

Pioneer Inn, the town's estimable and elderly hotel is at its nicest at dinner when you are invited to broil your own steak in the inner garden, sitting at candlelit tables under thatch umbrellas. Opt for prime ribs, *mahi-mahi* or fondue, if you prefer. Salad from a counter and barbecued baked beans are included. The Inn also serves breakfast and lunch. All meals are, by and large, *budget.*

The Rusty Harpoon is another broil-your-own dinner spot, offering pork chops, *mahi-mahi* or hamburgers. There are sandwiches and salads for lunch, and the drinks of which the house is proudest are its daiquiris, especially the banana ones. Another drink—the Doc Baldwin—is named in irreverent jest for the pioneer missionary whose house is a major sight-seer's destination, and who just had to be a teetotaler. *Budget.*

The Whale's Tale is a nautical look, upstairs gallery open to the breezes and the harbor. Very attractive with a fairly diverse menu running the chicken, spareribs, steak, seafood gamut. *Moderate.*

Elsewhere on Maui

Buzz's (Maalaea Bay) is, with good reason, a favorite of Maui residents. The local fish is excellent, and so is the steak and lobster platter. On Sundays there are queues for the 24-ounce servings of prime ribs of beef. Delicious home-baked bread. *Expensive.*

Chez Paul (Olowalu) has a deceptively simple exterior. Within is an authentic French restaurant that packs 'em in with solid bourgeois cooking. Book first. *Moderate.*

Kula Lodge is a mountain retreat at a 3,200-foot altitude near Haleakala National Park. It's usually cool enough, sunshine notwithstanding, for there to be a need for an open fire, even at lunch. Stop for that meal enroute to the park (service can be slow and food pedestrian, but the view—and that fireplace—compensate) or for breakfast if you've made an early trip to see the sun rise at Haleakala. *Moderate.*

Maalaea Bay Store (Maalaea Bay): The best darned hot dogs on the island of Maui; stop in for one when you're driving past. *Budget.*

Wailea Steak House (Wailea Golf Course): Located within the golf course's clubhouse, and open to the public, the lure here is a very good dinner—and not only the steak which gives the place its name. Liked by locals. *Moderate.*

SELECTED KAUAI RESTAURANTS

Casi di Grillo (Haleko Shopping Center, Lihue) is a charming Italian place, with a variety of pasta dishes—lasagna, cannelloni, spaghetti, and other specialties including chicken cacciatore and pork parmigiana. Lunches are simpler. *Moderate.*

Club Jetty is situated way at the end of a long pier at the foot of the hill on which the Kauai Surf Hotel is located. "Mama," the proprietor, turns out tasty Chinese chow. *Moderate.*

The Coconut Palace at Coco Palms Hotel, is its smartest restaurant. (The restaurant to avoid here is the massive Lagoon Dining Room with inept service and tasteless fare, albeit a splendid nightly show starring local talent.) The Coconut Palace is something else again, featuring prime ribs, steak and complete Chinese dinners, as well. *Expensive.*

The Fisherman (on the grounds of, but detached from the Kauai Surf Hotel) is an atmospheric seafood restaurant—local catches of the day, broiled *mahi-mahi,* imported lobster. *Expensive.*

The Golden Cape (Kauai Surf Hotel) is its top-of-the-tower room, and about as elegant a locale as one will come across on Kauai. The appointments are handsome, the food—steaks, ribs, poultry, seafood—tasty and the service thoroughly delightful. *Expensive.*

Kauai Resort Hotel Restaurant: Big, high-ceilinged, vibrant and a favorite with the locals. Dinner is agreeable, especially so the one night of the week (usually Monday) when a Chinese buffet is featured. *Moderate–Expensive.*

J.J.'s Boiler Room (Coconut Plantation) and **J.J.'s Boiler** (Haleko Shopping Center, Lihue) are a pair of solid-value steak houses. With your meat course, you help yourself to salads in wide variety from a buffet; hot garlic bread and coffee accompany. And everything tastes good. Friendly service. *Moderate.*

Plantation Gardens (Poipu Beach) is a restaurant occupying a lovely old house in the midst of a perfectly beautiful garden, in itself worthy of a fairly leisurely perusal. The lunch menu is so abbreviated as to be rather dull, but dinner is interesting and runs a wide gamut—steaks, seafood, even cannelloni and *coq-au-vin,* with Hawaiian *lomi-lomi* salmon and *poi* available as appetizers. Gracious service. *Moderate* for lunch; *expensive* for dinner.

Reuben's (Coconut Plantation) is quite as satisfactory on Kauai as on the Big Island and Oahu. The specialties are steaks, as well as broiled chicken and fish. Good desserts, too. And handsome surroundings. Breakfast, as well as lunch and dinner. *Moderate.*

The Rice Mill can be a sensible selection if you are up north at scenic Hanalei. The management is proud of its homemade breads, and soups, and such entrées as *teriyaki* pork chops and beef pie. There are steaks, of course, and at lunch the menu is simpler—those house soups, salads and sandwiches utilizing the baked-on-the-premises bread. *Moderate*.

Sugar Mill Snacks (Coconut Plantation) is conveniently located in the Coconut Plantation shopping complex. Good for breakfast, for lunch (the sandwiches are very good), and for snacks, especially if you are an ice cream nut; flavors include macadamia nut, Kona coffee and coconut. *Budget*.

5

Hawaii to Sip and Spectate

VARIATIONS ON A MOSTLY POLYNESIAN THEME

It is a tribute to the collective warmth and jollity of the Hawaiian personality that commercial entertainment thrives as it does, most especially on Oahu, but on the Neighbor Islands, as well. No major world resort of the calibre of Hawaii gets by on fewer imported big names. Show biz entrepreneurs have it made. If it is true that Norwegians are born on skis, Hawaiians are born with singing voices (some, to be sure, more melodious than others) ukuleles—or at least guitars—in their arms; limitless wardrobes of aloha shirts and muumuus, as the case may be; and perhaps most important, good looks coupled with the most infectious smiles on the planet.

A consequence of these mostly natural endowments is that live entertainment is at every turn. Even the least pretentious bar and the least celebrated hotel lounge will turn up with something to serenade one by, from cocktails onwards. So that if you get bored with the music where you're staying, eating, drinking or spectating, move along a few yards or at most a few hundred yards, and you've another bit of entertainment to appraise.

This vast amusement scene breaks itself down into categories. There are the commercial hotel *luaus,* the big hotel shows, the theater-style productions, some of which go on season after season, and the more intimate kind music in the bars and lounges; very often this last-mentioned is the most fun of the lot.

Allowing for variations and changes, here is a selective survey—mind you, I said *selective*—of the entertainment scene.

LUAUS

Ideally, the good-natured first-timer in Hawaii looks upon the *luau* as his initiation, the price he pays for an absolutely super Hawaiian holiday. The *luau*, as you will surely have heard in advance of your arrival, is the ancient Hawaiian feast translated into money-making mass-production merriment. It invariably takes place on a hotel beach, at dusk, with flaming torches providing the illumination. Everyone wears Hawaiian clothes—the men, aloha shirts; the ladies, muumuus. Admission includes a *hei* (floral headband), or a *lei* (floral necklace), and begins with cocktails at an open bar. What you want to determine before you sign up is whether or not this open bar provides *only* rum punches, or whether you have a choice of standard bar drinks—highballs, cocktails, or whatever, made to your order, as well as the sweetish punch. After a drink or two you are seated at long planklike tables. Great leaves from native plants take the place of crockery. But before eating, you watch the *Imu* ceremony—the removal of the roast *kalua* pig from its in-the-sand oven. A decorous torch-lighting ritual ensues, with scantily clad runner-lighters darting about illuminating the *heiau,* or sacred ground. (The beach, in other words.) You are then ready for dinner, for better or for worse. It is bound to include, as a minimum, chunks of the pig you witnessed being roasted, *lomi-lomi*—marinated—salmon, and *poi,* the starch staple whose basis is the taro plant. If you are lucky—and this is a happy current trend—you will also have a choice of more familiar foods, such as broiled fish (often the native—and delicious *mahi-mahi*) and barbecued chicken. But you are still not through. More entertainment follows, Hawaiian style. If you are a photographer, have flashbulbs at the ready and snap away. If your *luau* is of the kind with only the traditional Hawaiian staples, you may well still be hungry; many *luau* guests are. A hamburger at the nearest hotel coffee shop will set you up.

Now then, which *luau?* Here are a trio I've selected, each at an especially beautiful hotel. I am as sentimental as the next guy. The first *luau* I ever attended was at the **Royal Hawaiian Hotel;** it is no less corny than the others, but the setting is so lovely you can't help but enjoy yourself. It is among the more traditional of the hotel *luaus;* the Royal, after all goes back to the twenties.

The **Hawaiian Regent Hotel** has no beach that it can properly call its own, so it begins its *luau* with open-bar drinks on the third floor *lanai,* beach view, where pretty hulamaids greet guests with a *lei* and a kiss. The party then moves to the ballroom, and— please note—the food is among the tastiest of that served at the town's *luaus,* running to sweet-and-sour pork, chicken with rice, *teriyaki* steak and coconut cake.

The **Kahala Hilton** calls its *luau* a *hukilau, huki* meaning pull and *lau* the *ti*-leaf-covered rope attached to traditional Hawaiian fishing nets. Setting is the hotel's Hala Cove and its beach, and the evening is essentially a fishing party as of yore, but with Hilton International touches. The food is super—Island-style steak and fish, with a groaning buffet laden with all manner of more familiar taste treats as well. And the crowd—all decked out in floral *leis*— watches as the *hukilau* nets are lowered into the sea from a traditional canoe, and later, pulled aboard the craft and brought to the beach, as guests' cameras record the action. A show—dancing and singing—follows.

SPLASHY SHOWS

Monarch Room, Royal Hawaiian Hotel: Grand for dinner (Chapter 3), grand—in the traditional style—for a high-impact floor show, and dancing.

Hala Terrace, Kahala Hilton Hotel: Casual setting, top entertainment; traditionally a requisite destination.

Bora Bora Room, Waikiki Beachcomber Hotel: Nightly Polynesian-style revues.

Hawaiian Hut, Ala Moana Hotel: An action-packed show, dinner, and late-late dancing.

Canoe House, Ilikai Hotel: First-rate entertainment, dinner dancing.

Polynesian Palace, Reef Towers Hotel: About as essential for first-timers as a *luau:* Buffet dinner and two shows per evening.

Sheraton-Waikiki Hotel Swimming Pool: A water ballet (remember Esther Williams?) following a buffet supper; traditionally on Thursday, but you had better double-check.

DANCE AWAY THE EVENING

Beef 'n' Grog (Royal Block, Kalakaua Avenue): Good music for dancing, usually from 10:30 P.M. onwards—way onwards.

The Point After (Hawaiian Regent Hotel) just has to be the smartest disco in town, from 9 P.M. until very late.

JB's (Colony Surf East Hotel): Crowded, modish and fun. Tardy arrivals recommended.

Hawaiian Hut (Ala Moana Hotel): At 11 P.M., after the floor show is over, this place becomes a groovy dance palace.

Mike's (Beach Walk): The broil-your-own kitchen closes at 11 P.M. and the name of the game becomes dancing.

Tiki (International Market Place): Sardine-packed, with youngish dancers enjoying the beat; after 10:30 P.M. nightly.

THEATER, CONCERTS, MOVIES, PORNO

Chaminade College Theatre (3140 Waeiae Avenue, not far from Waikiki): Frequent presentations of plays.

Heritage Theatre (King's Alley Shopping Center): Hawaiian history, pageant style and live, of course, presented under the auspices of the Bernice P. Bishop Museum.

Hilton Dome (Hilton Hawaiian Village Hotel complex): A spectacular variation on the Hawaiian-history theme, in a spectacular setting; the stage is the largest in the state.

Honolulu International Center Arena: Watch the papers and the what's-on-magazines, for current attractions. A regular tenant is the estimable *Honolulu Symphony Orchestra,* which also performs in the Waikiki Shell (see below).

Hula Shows: Waikiki Shell (Kapiolani Park) (adult dancers) and Ala Moana Shopping Center (the dancers are kids). Check for performance dates and times; no charge.

Kennedy Theatre (University of Hawaii): Plays and other events; watch the press for specifics.

Movies: The handsome *Waikiki* on Kalakaua Avenue is the most convenient cinema for most visitors. There are, of course, many others. Watch the papers.

Porno: Several Hotel Street theaters feature live nudie shows. Perhaps more unusual (*Variety*'s coverage did no harm) has been the scene at *Dunes* out near the airport; its naked waiters are the stars of its stage show every evening, and some days even at lunchtime.

Royal Hawaiian Band Concerts: Kapiolani Park and Iolani Palace Bandstand; no charge.

TELEVISION

There are five channels. Their numbers—in Honolulu—are 2 (KHON-NBC); 4 (ABC), 9 (KGMB-CBS), 11 (KHET-Educational), and 13 (KIKU, independent). The daily papers have programs.

COCKTAIL LOUNGES

There are ways and ways of visiting the interesting hotels. One is to live in them; another is to dine at them; still a third is to pop in for breakfast. These have all been dealt with on earlier pages. There remains the business of taking in their shows, and, last, of darting in for a drink or two. Bars and lounges usually open at 11 A.M. and offer entertainment from cocktail time onwards. Here are some that I like:

Views of the beach:
>Surf Room Bar, Royal Hawaiian Hotel;
>Michel's, Colony Surf Hotel;
>Garden Bar, Hilton Hawaiian Village,
>Gangplank Lounge, Surfrider Hotel.

Views from on high:
>Summit Lounge, Ala Moana Hotel;
>Hanohano Room, Sheraton-Waikiki Hotel;
>Top of the I, Ilikai Hotel.

Poolside drinks:
>Kahala Hilton;
>Kuhio Hotel Warrior Bar—and with complimentary *puupuus.*

Indoor atmosphere:

> Davy Jones' Locker, Reef Hotel (with a see-through wall into the pool);
>
> Lobby Lounge, Hawaiian Regent Hotel;
>
> Kon Tiki Lounge, Sheraton-Waikiki Hotel.

Cocktails and

Dinner at Sea:

> Windjammer Cruises' sailing vessels depart from Fisherman's Wharf, usually twice each evening, serve dinner as well as drinks.
>
> Hilton Hawaiian Village's catamaran sails each evening on a cocktail-dinner cruise.

6

Hawaii to Play

Combine the Hawaiian beaches with the waters adjacent to them and add the equable climate. It is not difficult to consider how well the athlete and sportsman fares in these islands. If one leaves aside swimming, the major visitor-sport is golf. (There are some forty courses.) Tennis follows. Deep-sea fishing is popular, too. And so are all of the water-allied sports—snorkling, scuba diving and most especially surfing, which is, after all, a Hawaiian-origin sport.

GOLF

The great majority of the courses are on Oahu, but there are some not-to-be missed beauties on the Neighbor Islands. It is difficult, for that matter, to find a course without a scenic setting. No area in the world that I know of has a higher concentration of magnificently situated golf links. If you're a member of a golf or country club at home, bring your card along, to arrange for courtesy privileges at the private clubs in Hawaii. Here are some of the outstanding courses that are open to the public.

Oahu

Ala Wai Golf Course fringes the canal that constitutes Waikiki's *mauka* frontier. Very convenient for visitors; 18 holes, par 71.

Hawaii Kai is a pair of courses, near Koko Head, which is just beyond Diamond Head. One is championship (18 holes, par 72), the other executive (18 holes, par 56).

Pali Golf Course is at the foot of the Pali Lookout, at Kaneohe; 18 holes, par 72.

Makaha Country Club's pair of courses are on the scenic *ewa,* or west coast of the island; both are 18 holes, par 72.

The Big Island of Hawaii

Mauna Kea Beach Hotel's 18-hole course is among the more magnificently situated—anywhere—and was designed by Robert Trent Jones; 18 holes, par 72.

The Volcano House Golf Course straddles exciting terrain of Hawaii Volcanoes National Park, near Hilo; 18 holes, par 72.

Keauhou-Kona Golf Course is ideal for Kona Coast visitors; 18 holes, par 72.

Maui

The Royal Kaanapali Golf Course is another masterfully designed Robert Trend Jones links, splendidly situated on a bluff above Kaanapali Beach, its hotels, and the Pacific; 18 holes, par 72.

Wailea Golf Course has a lovely setting; 18 holes, par 72.

Kauai

The Wailua Golf Course is considered to be one of the best in Hawaii; 18 holes, par 72.

Kauai Surf Hotel Golf Course borders a bluff above the sea; 18 holes, par 72.

Molokai

Iron Hills is operated by the Del Monte Corporation; 9 holes, par 35.

Lanai

Cavendish Golf Course is celebrated state-wide, thanks to its lack of green fees; 9 holes, par 36.

TENNIS

Tennis in Hawaii, as just about everywhere, becomes increasingly popular. Most courts are of good quality—of Laykold or Plexipave asphalt-type surfaces. Public courts everywhere are the baliwick of the county Parks and Recreations Departments, and they are free, on a first-come, first-served basis. Demand is heaviest, not unsurprisingly on courts in and around *Waikiki Beach,* Oahu. The most conveniently located courts in that area are those of Kapiolani Tennis Center, Diamond Head Tennis Center, Koko Head Tennis Center, and Ala Moana Park. Newest of the hotel courts are those on the roof of the Ilikai. On the *Big Island of Hawaii,* there are public courses in and around Kailua-Kona

and Hilo and at several hotels, including the Mauna Kea Beach
Hotel. On *Maui,* there are public courts in Wailuku and Lahaina,
and at hotels including the Maui Surf, Napili Kai Beach Club,
Royal Lahaina and Sheraton-Maui. *Kauai* has public courts in
Lihue and at other points, and at hotels including the Kauai Surf,
Kauai Beach Boy, and Princeville at Hanalei. *Molokai* and *Lanai*
have public courts, too.

DEEP-SEA FISHING

The Hawaiian seas are chock-a-block full of game fish, and
there is organized charter-fishing on all of the major islands. But
fish first. What you'll catch, if you're lucky, are tuna (Hawaiian:
ahi), Bonito (*aku*), Barracuda (*kaku*), Marlin (*a'u*), Dolphin
(*mahi-mahi*) and Wahoo (*ono*).

Oahu and the Kona Coast of the Big Island of Hawaii are the
most reputed fishing centers. On Oahu, boats depart mainly from
Fisherman's Wharf (also known as Kewalo Basin) but also from
Barber's Point, Kaneohe Bay, Waianae and Penguin Banks.
There are charter boats, also, at Kona on the Big Island, Lahaina,
Maui and Hanalei, Kauai, to name but three points. And remem-
ber: no seasons, no deep-sea fishing licenses, no fishing limits.

SURFING

Surfing goes back to the ancient Hawaiians, and although the
missionaries were responsible for putting a stop to the sport
(they were agin' it because the people placed bets—enormous
bets—on it), modern Hawaiians revived it in the early years of
this century. The locale was Waikiki Beach, right where it all began.

Look out of your Waikiki hotel window and you'll note several
frothy-wave surfing areas. They all have names, and their location

and strength play a major role in the sport. The calmest surf is
called Malihini (the word for newcomer, and applied to us on our
first visits); it's where learners get the hang of things. As one goes
out into the sea, one sees Canoe, the major area, with the closest-
to-perfect waves. Farther out are the Kuna waves, with Public
Bath and Castle Surf the most distant. The nine- to twelve-foot
boards that the surfies use today are rentable through beach hotels (through which one may arrange for instruction), and so for
that matter are the impedimenta of such water sports as scuba
diving, snorkeling and outrigger-canoeing. But the most Hawaiian
of the lot is surfing. Arise early and you'll see its practitioners—
youngsters for many of whom the sport is a passion, a way of life
—riding the waves as soon as the sun rises, remaining until it
sets.

7

Hawaii to Buy

THE PERSPECTIVE ON SHOPPING

You no more intend shopping, to any appreciable extent, in Hawaii than you contemplate lessons in the hula—or skin diving. Nonetheless, all are not only possible, but probable on a holiday in the Islands. The point to remember straight off is that there are no bargains to speak of. Prices on most things are more or less what they would be at home. You shop because shopping is an intrinsic part of holiday life in Hawaii as at any resort. Designers and manufacturers are well aware of this. Devilishly clever, they have promoted their wares so as to make the visitor feel just a little out of things if he isn't wearing a bold-patterned aloha shirt instead of the perfectly nice sport shirt he brought from home. Or if his wife isn't wearing a locally made muumuu instead of the smart long shift she had in her suitcase. Carry that through to costume jewelry (for men as well as women), footwear, bathing suits and other beachwear, even including Hawaiian-made suntan lotion, and one appreciates how sugar, pineapple and the hotel business are competing with a series of relatively new industries that contribute considerably to the economy of State No. 50.

Aside from purchases made on the scene for one's own use,

there remains the matter of gifts for the folks back home. Our hosts are no slouches in this area either.

The U. S. Agriculture Department allows us to take home *leis*—the floral necklaces with which both men and women are festooned; paper thin, flaming red Bougainvillia, carnations in pink and red and white, tiny orchids, fragrant gardenias, fragile plumeria. Not to mention shell and seed *leis,* both the bargain-cheap ones—*koa haole* they're called—and the surprisingly costly *kukui* nut ones—glossy, ebony-colored and a favorite with men, worn over aloha shirts for dressy evenings.

The *clothes* we buy for ourselves—aloha shirts, especially the modified safari-jacket style, and swimsuits for men; muumuus of varying styles, and shifts for women, as well as swimwear and children's wear—are transported across the Pacific to the Mainland in considerable quantities.

So is *costume jewelry,* not only the above-mentioned seed and nut *leis,* but necklaces, bracelets, rings, earrings of native materials like black and red coral, semi-precious olivine, shells and imported jade and ivory.

Handicrafts are often more machine- than handmade,—and are not always local. Still, they broadly include bowls, platters and trays of monkeypod and koa wood; ceramics in various guises, bambooware, gimmicky and tacky things made out of coconut shells, and—rest assured—grass hula skirts for the kids.

Hawaii has entered the *perfume-cologne-after-shave* industry and with considerable success. Women who know and love French perfumes are not likely to take the Pacific variations on this theme too seriously. Still, if the perfumes tend to be too sweetly floral, the lighter toilet waters can be refreshing and gift-worthy. And the for-men-only branch of this industry has had more success: The great majority of the men's colognes and after-shaves are brisk, citrusy, uncloying and agreeable, making excellent gifts.

Hawaiian *things to eat and drink* are invariably welcome back home. The islands' own pineapples are available in special packages which airport shops will ship to any overseas destination. Macadamia nuts make good gifts although they are rarely less ex-

pensive (try the supermarkets and big department stores) than
on the Mainland. Hawaiian fruits are made into jams and jellies.
Kona coffee is a delicious albeit luxurious gift. Candies made of
Hawaiian ingredients, mostly coconut and macadamia nuts and
can be delicious. (Ed & Don's Macadamia Nut Bars—chocolate
covered—are wickedly habit forming, if one is not careful. So are
the cellophane bags of Hawaiian Candy's Coconut Brittle. And
the limitless species of Chinese dried fruits—called "crack seeds"
locally—are delicious.) Surprise packages might well contain Hawaiian liqueurs—with Kona coffee, passion fruit and pineapple
bases; or Hawaiian-distilled vodka, rum and even *sake.*

To be considered too, are *books* on Hawaiian history and culture—these are available in abundant variety, along with *paintings and drawings* by resident artists.

ABOUT THE SHOPS IN THIS BOOK

Shopping in Hawaii is heavily centered on the shopping center.
This is the case, even in urban areas, where centers are easily
reached by public transport, or by foot. Tremendous emphasis is
placed on ambience. The shopping centers are among the most
beautiful anywhere in the United States. And this can obtain in
the Neighbor Islands—Whalers Village on Maui is a good example—as well as in Honolulu.

What follow are a *selection*—just a selection—of shops that I
find worthwhile in major shopping areas on the major islands. For
the shopper's convenience, they are arranged first by area, and
then by category.

SELECTED HONOLULU SHOPS

It is as well to begin in this metropolitan center, with a break-
down on the principal shopping areas. In *Waikiki,* where most
visitors headquarter, *Kalakaua Avenue,* the main thoroughfare,

is the site of many shops, but several shopping centers branch off from it. These include the *Rainbow Bazaar,* embracing a considerable quantity of shops in a rather gaudy Chinese-design complex of the Hilton Hawaiian Village; the *International Market Place* in the heart of Waikiki, which I find more interesting for its restaurants and dancing spots (see Chapters 4, 5) than for its shops; and *King's Alley,* highlights of which I describe in later paragraphs.

Beyond Waikiki, in the fashionable *Kahala* area, one finds *Kahala Mall* which is worth inspecting if only because it is so grand—with its enclosed air-conditioned and carpeted passageways; the only Hawaiian outlet of the California-origin Joseph Magnin specialty-shop chain, and handsome branches of such stores as Liberty House, J. C. Penney, McInerny, and Woolworth's, not to mention a Star Supermarket, and a number of smart smaller shops. Kahala Mall is nicely combined with a visit to the not-far-distant Kahala Hilton.

Up the east coast, enroute to attractions like the Blow Hole (Chapter 2), is *Koko Marina Waterfront Village,* overlooking a capacious marina, and constituting a collection of charming shops with a salty waterfront ambience. Wares range from hand-tooled leather through beaded necklaces and hand-wrought copperware, with tropical fish and Oriental food-treats also present. There are special Koko Marina bus departures from Waikiki a number of times daily.

Downtown Honolulu's principal emporia are centered in the *Fort Street Mall.* There remain other centers of import: relatively small *Kilohana Square,* where the emphasis is on handicrafts and antiques, and Ala Moana Shopping Center, in and of itself a major Honolulu destination for the visitor, be he a shopper, browser or, for that matter, absolute skinflint.

ALA MOANA SHOPPING CENTER

Ala Moana is nothing less than a mercantile pearl of the Pacific. What we are talking about here are 155 shops, restaurants and service establishments set in a multi-level, fifty-acre complex that delights the eye with carp-filled ponds, striking sculpture, and public areas alive with entertainments ranging from kids' hula shows to oomp-bah-band concerts. Ala Moana is Honolulu's answer to the forum of ancient Rome. The newcomer does well to pick up a diagram of the place at the information center, upon arrival. But Honolulans of all ages know Ala Moana inside and out. And love it. You get there by car (there is an enormous 7,800-space parking area), or by Bus No. 8 from Waikiki. The whole place is usually open through until 9 P.M. Monday through Friday, 5:30 P.M. on Saturday, 4 P.M. on Sundays.

There's a post office, two branch banks, taxi stand, shoe-repair shop, gas station, dry cleaners, locksmith all on the premises. There are a number of recommendable restaurants (see Chapter 4) and of the scores of shops, here are some that I like.

Books

Honolulu Book Shop: Big, browseworthy, with lots of paperbacks and a good Hawaiiana section.

Clothing

Cook's Bay: Among the smarter apparel shops in the Honolulu area, with things to wear for kids, teens and men as well. The Hawaiian-design things are the ones to concentrate on.

Hartfield's: The specialty is budget-priced women's clothes, just the place to pick up that extra muumuu.

Kramer's: Men's and boy's wear, practical and well-priced rather than high-styled; white slacks and jeans of all types are a specialty. Aloha shirts and swimsuits, too.

McInerny, Ltd.: One of Honolulu's oldest and most respected men's clothiers. (I remember buying my first Hawaiian swimsuit at McInerny's during World War II.) Handsome Hawaiian-design shirts, safari jackets and a full range of slacks and accessories.

Seafarer makes a specialty of leatherware—sandals, belts, even hats, for both men and women.

Walter Clarke's bag is resort wear for the ladies—muumuus in varying lengths and styles; and kids' clothing, too.

Department and Variety Stores

Liberty House, the leading Hawaiian department store (and a part of the Amfac conglomerate, along with Island Holidays hotels, Joseph Magnin, and Maui's Royal Kaanapali golf course, among much else), is at its beautiful best in Ala Moana. This is what department-store design should be all about. The men's department is on the main floor—and includes a generous section with Hawaiian duds. All of the women's departments are upstairs. Books, toys and housewares are in the basement. The restaurant is worthy of mention in Chapter 4. And there is a shop-by-mail service: If you've forgotten something or want to re-order, write Laura Hale, Liberty House Shopping Service, P. O. Box 2690, Honolulu, Hawaii 96803.

J. C. Penney, plainer, of course, than Liberty House, is full of good buys for the visitor. The Hawaiian gifts department on the main floor is one of extraordinary variety—dolls, shells, perfumes, costume jewelry, monkeypod and koa wood trays, place mats, pineapple and guava jellies and jams, coconut candies . . . to give you an idea. Women's Clothing is very big on muumuus, and Men's Clothing is equally generous in its stocks of aloha shirts and accessories, at some of the most attractive prices in town.

Sears, Roebuck is a neat triple-level emporium. In the basement, note the orchid plants and fresh flowers (these may be taken to the Mainland) as well as the Hawaiian foodstuffs—jams, candies and the like. Still additional souvenirs are to be found on the main floor along with books, and both men's and women's Hawaiian clothing at attractive prices.

Shirokiya is a transplanted Japanese department store, not a whit less authentic than prototypes back on home territory. All of the smells and sounds and signs of Nippon make a visit here a delightful bit of Instant Japan. There's an enormous Noritake china department, books and magazines all in Japanese, lacquerware and sake-serving sets, happi coats, an antiques section with splendid Samuraii swords and delicate porcelain, and most fun of all, the food departments, with demonstrators all about, and assortments of such staples as noodles, tea, soy sauce, frozen fish (how about some whale fillets?) and pickled vegetables. Plan to give this one some time.

Woolworth's is big and with diverse range of departments, from aloha shirts and muumuus to fresh papaya and pizza, these last purchased by shoppers who take them outside and munch them while seated on benches. Woolworth's restaurant facilities are highlighted in Chapter 4.

Food Stores

Crack Seed Center is a Chinese candy store full of treats for the newcomer to this kind of confectionery. What you must do is make a purchase of two or three or four, for tasting purposes. And go on from there. There are preserved plums, persimmons and mangoes, pickled apricots and peaches, sweet cherry preserves and sweet-and-sour lemon peel, ginger in sixteen varieties, and such savory treats as soy-flavored crackers, hot-seasoned clams, dried cuttlefish and shrimp.

Ed & Don's Ice Cream Parlor: a branch of an Island-wide chain; everything is very good.

McDonald's Doughnut Shop: Doughnuts in limitless variety, including frostings of local ingredients, like pineapple, coconut and macadamia nuts.

Foodland Supermarket: Stock up on nibbles to have with drinks on the *lanai* of your hotel room, picnic provisions, or whatever. If you like macadamia nuts, supermarkets usually sell them for less than Waikiki shops; look for the jars of broken ones—they taste quite as good as the whole nuts, but they're cheaper.

Jewelry and Paintings

Security Diamond: The specialties are a type of jewelry beloved of the locals. It's called Hawaiian Heirloom, and it's made of gold in the fashion of a century or so ago. Names are usually inscribed in Hawaiian, with legends like "kuupio" (sweetheart), "aloha" or simply one's initials. Nice gifts or mementos.

A-A Jewelry and Antiques: You wouldn't realize it from the name, but this is a super source of Thai Buddha figures, mostly elderly, and of good quality. Other Thai pieces, too. The jewelry includes fine pearls.

Gima's Art Gallery: Have a look at contemporary paintings by Island artists.

Records

House of Music Ltd.: Just the place to pick up the records of Hawaiian artists that have become your favorites. Tapes, sheet music, guitars, ukuleles—the works.

Shoes

The Slipper House: Convenient if you've forgotten to bring a pair of sandals with you, or need an extra pair. Baskets and tote bags, too. Inexpensive.

Souvenirs and Gifts

Myrna Loy is no relation to the actress of that name, but is a shop worth knowing about if one's interests run to articles carved from koa and monkeypod wood—bowls, trays, figures, of good quality if not necessarily of high style.

Philippine Handicrafts: Everything is from the Philippines—the men's shirts of pineapple fiber known as *barong tagalogs,* woodenware, shells, woven mats. And tasteful.

KING'S ALLEY SHOPPING CENTER

The Hawaii of the late nineteenth-century monarchy—gay and festive and evocative, with live music each evening along with a daily Changing of the Guard, as it was when Kalakaua was king. Usually open until 11:00 P.M. every day, with half a hundred shops and services, my favorites of which are as follows:

Food Stores

ABC Discount: Actually not a part of the King's Alley complex, but included at this point because it is on Kaiulani Avenue, just next door, and because it is a first-rate source of groceries, snacks and sundries—perhaps that tube of tooth paste you forgot to pack, or something to nibble on with your sunset cocktails.

Island Candy & Gourmet Shop: Just what the name implies. All kinds of tempters. By the box for gifts, bars for immediate sustenance (Ed & Don's Macadamia Nut Bars, for example) and bags of delicious sweets, including Hawaii Candy's Coconut Brittle.

Sundae Palace: Gooey sundaes and other frozen concoctions, or just plain ice cream, if you're a purist.

Clothing and Fabrics

Crazy Shirts, Inc.: T-shirts in all sizes and hues and with all manner of legends and designs imprinted upon them.

Fabrics of the Pacific, Inc.: If you like the cotton and part-cotton materials used for the manufacture of aloha shirts and muumuus, here's where you can buy them by the yard.

Harriet's will make up muumuus, caftans, aloha shirts—what have you—in the fabric you select from an enormous stock, and have it ready in two days. Smart ready-made, too.

Liberty House: A small outpost of the department store group, mostly with clothing and accessories, both men's and women's.

Hawaiiana

Bishop Museum Gift Shop: A branch of the main shop in the museum (see Chapter 2) and full of worthwhile mementos of the islands—books on Hawaiian history and culture, and a great variety of well-crafted objects, with tapa cloths a specialty.

Jewelry

The Carat Patch is a cleverly titled jewelry shop, with its wares quite as imaginative as its name. The look is contemporary.

WAIKIKI'S KALAKAUA AVENUE

Liberty House: This good-looking branch of the Hawaii-wide department store chain is not as impressive as the earlier-recommended Ala Moana store, or the one at Kahala Mall. Still, it includes departments of special interest to the Waikiki visitor, with excellent selections in all of them—women's clothing and accessories, men's clothing and accessories, and Hawaiian gifts (woodenware, jams and jellies, bambooware, ceramics, books, perfumes and colognes). The salespeople are invariably helpful.

Ming's (2295 Kalakaua Avenue) is a long-established jewelry store with a number of branches (including one on Fifth Avenue in New York). The traditional specialty is jade—earrings, necklaces, earclips, rings and larger objects as well, including antique bowls and figurines. There are less-expensive jewelry pieces, too —sandlewood necklaces from India, for example. A lovely shop.

McInerny, Ltd.: One of the bigger of the long-in-business McInerny shops, with quality men's clothing and accessories, much of it high-style, and the emphasis, not surprisingly, on Hawaiian designs.

Pauline Lake (Basement, Royal Hawaiian Hotel): A honey of a shop, this. Most of the wares are fine Oriental antiques, and contemporarily made smaller objects. But there are, as well, clothing and accessories for both men and women. The key word here is style. Very special.

Shellworld (Diamond Head wing, Moana Hotel): Species after species. They are mostly imports from the Philippines and northern Australia—and they come in a variety of species. Coral, too.

Sugar 'n Spice 'n Everything Nice (International Market Place): fudge, candy, nuts, all wickedly rich.

Woolworth's: As all-purpose as a Woolworth's can be, with the worth-noting grocery department with heat-and-serve foods (for visitors with kitchen facilities) a specialty. The restaurant is recommended in Chapter 4.

KILOHANA SQUARE SHOPPING CENTER

The lure here is handmade things, antiques and the like. A

favorite with residents. To get there, take Bus No. 2 Waikiki-Campbell; it runs on Kalakaua Avenue, and you want to go in the direction of Diamond Head.

Bamboo Needle: Needlepoint nuts—this is your Honolulu headquarters.

Carriage House: Antiques, mostly but not exclusively English.

Hand and Eye: All manner of contemporary creations, ceramics, clothes, metalwork, jewelry.

Exotic Siam: Thai imports, including some fine Buddha heads and figures—the latter both standing and reclining.

MUSEUM SHOPS

Bishop Museum Shop (1355 Kalihi Street): Not unlike the museum itself (Chapter 2), the shop's thrust is Hawaiiana, with other areas of the Pacific represented, too. The selection of books, of Hawaiian history and culture, is very good indeed. So are the museum's own post-card reproductions of its paintings of the Hawaiian monarchs and of early Hawaiians, especially those by the artists John Webber, who sailed with Captain Cook (1778–79), and R. Dampier, who painted a number of Hawaiians in 1825. Bigger than the earlier-recommended branch at Waikiki's King's Alley.

Mission Houses Museum Shop (553 South King Street): Contemporary scrimshaw—the carving on ivory and whalebone that the whaling crews used to do to pass away long months at sea—is available here. So are high-quality *leis* of *kukui* nuts, missionary dolls, Mission Houses T-shirts, feather *leis,* and a whopping big selection of books on Hawaiian history and culture, Hawaiian cookery, and Hawaiiana for the kids.

SELECTED BIG ISLAND SHOPS

Kailua-Kona

Art Gallery of the Kona Inn Shopping Center: Paintings and water colors, many on local themes, by area artists.

Blair's: An extensive selection of koa and monkeypod wood platters and bowls.

Ice 9: Hand-blown glass, paintings by Big Island artists.

Jug 'n' Jigger: Wine, liquor, Hawaiian colognes, perfumes and candies.

Kona Batik: Women's clothes, and with style.

Reyn's: A small branch (at the entrance of the Kona Inn) of the first-rate Neighbor Islands men's clothing chain.

K. Taniguchi: A dilly of a supermarket-general store, stocked with groceries, liquor, sundries and what all. The whole town shops and gossips here, as is evident from the bulletin board around the side, which I suggest perusing.

Hilo

Book Gallery (211 Knoole Street): One of the most interesting collections of Hawaiiana in the state; note the Hawaiian cookbooks.

S. H. Kress Co.: An exemplary branch of the well-known variety-store chain, with a convenient restaurant-fountain.

Lyman House Museum Shop (276 Haili Street): The selection of gifts, cards, crafts and books is tasteful and distinctive. The notepapers with Big Island quilt designs on their covers are noteworthy, no pun intended. So is the museum-published book, *Sarah Joiner Lyman of Hawaii: Her Own Story.*

Moo Moo Tree (Naniloa Surf Hotel): Women's resort togs in abundant variety.

Orchids of Hawaii (575 Hinano Street): One of a number of Hilo nurseries that specializes in the sale of locally grown flowers on the spot, and by mail to the Mainland. Available are anthuriums, birds of paradise, red ginger, wood roses, and varieties of orchids.

Waikea Resort Village Market Place: This is an adjunct of the Polynesian-style hotel recommended in Chapter 3, and embraces something like a score of shops, occupying low-rise peak-roofed buildings in a tropical garden of bamboo, palm trees, ginger blossoms and carp-filled ponds. Amble about and play your own favorites. Mine include *House of Bamboo* (coasters, baskets, trays), *Manila Bay Co.* (Philippine imports including Barong Tagalog shirts of pineapple-fiber cloth, and the so-called jellyfish-shell chandeliers); *Waiakea Gems* (jewelry of black coral, jade and pearl); *Tonga South Pacific Co.* (tapa cloth, shell *leis,* New Hebrides figures, other exotica); *Reyn's*—one of the bigger branches of the exemplary high-style Neighbor Islands men's wear chains (their safari-style coat jackets are especially recommended); *Vagabond Shells; The Muumuu Tree* women's clothes; and *Flowers by Keahoha*—which ships Big Island orchids and other flowers to the Mainland, as well as selling them on the spot. There is always a stock of the cheapest-species orchid, the Joaquin; they cost about a quarter per blossom. *Snack spots* are on the grounds, for refreshment pauses.

SELECTED MAUI SHOPS

Kahului

Maui Mall: The works—all wrapped up in a handsome shopping center, with such draws as *Long's Drugs, Star Supermarket,* and for an Italian lunch—the *Pizza Factory.*

Lahaina

Baldwin House Bookshop (Front Street): A worthy enterprise of the Lahaina Restoration Foundation, which runs the next-door house, as well. Books, cards, prints, other articles with an Old Lahaina twist.

Court House: The building is more than a century old, but contemporarily sees service as a gallery for the works of local painters, many on Maui themes.

Ed & Don's (Pioneer Inn): A convenient outpost of the Island-wide ice-cream chain.

Ned Briggs (Front Street): Attractive men's wear.

South Seas Trading Post (Front Street): Quality handicraft imports from the Solomons, Tonga, New Guinea, Fiji, Tahiti and northern Australia.

The Wardrobe (Pioneer Inn): Hawaiian togs for the ladies.

Kaanapali Beach

Reyn's (Royal Lahaina Hotel): The Maui branch of the Neighbor Islands men's wear chain; good-looking resort wear.

South Seas Trading Post (Royal Lahaina Hotel): A branch of the same shop described above in Lahaina.

Whalers Village: After Ala Moana in Honolulu, Whalers Village is quite the most beautiful shopping center in the state. The "whaler" in the title relates to the museum part of the center. Scattered throughout the nine-acre site are nearly one hundred out-in-the-open and glass-encased exhibits—the jaws of a sperm whale, an antique sea chest, a whale boat, some fine scrimshaw—that tell the story of this region's whaling past. There are a number of restaurants (see Chapter 4) and, needless to say, shops. Of the score-plus, my favorites include: a honey of a branch of *Liberty House* department store (Whalers Village, like Liberty House, is a part of the Amfac conglomerate); the *Sea Scoop Ice Cream Parlor* (for banana and macadamia-nut waffles at breakfast); *Gear-Up,* a mod-clothes—very smart and with-it—affiliate of Liberty House; *The Book Cache*—a very comfortable repository of printed matter; *Ka Honu,* with South Pacific craft imports and super scrimshaw; paintings by Maui artists—often on local themes—in the *Village Gallery;* and comestibles, in the *Village Deli*. There are a *movie theater,* and an *amphitheater* at which frequent free entertainments are staged.

SELECTED KAUAI SHOPS

Coconut Plantation's Market Place is an agreeable maze of shops, services, restaurants (Chapter 4) and hotels (Chapter 3) near Kapaa. Shops that I like include an attractive branch of *Liberty House* department store, mostly with resort wear; *Coco Resort Shop* (well-priced muumuus and aloha shirts); *Guadalupe,* whose elaborate original designs have a considerable following; *Hale Hana,* with handmade Kauai crafts; and the *Plantation Pantry* (groceries).

Kauai Museum Shop (Lihue) is a tempting jumble of books of Hawaiiana, cards, notepaper, featuring reproductions of old Kauai quilt designs, and other Kausiana.

Kay O'Kauai (Coco Palms Hotel and other locations) is an all-the-family resort shop, with an auxiliary gift line, as well, and a special custom-service whereby whatever garment you order is ready in twenty-four hours.

Lihue Shopping Center, in the center of Lihue, is a good all-round source for purchases. Emporia that I recommend include *Lihue Stores,* a capacious department store that is a part of the Amfac group and has substantial men's, women's and kids' resort-wear departments, and gifts, as well; *Sears,* with budget-priced resort wear for both men and women; and a big *Woolworth's* with all-the-family resort-clothing and gift departments as well as a restaurant.

Reyn's Men's Wear (Kauai Surf Hotel) is a branch of the Neighbor Islands chain that has the smartest men's aloha togs in Hawaii.

The Tourist Trap out on the island, at the junction of Koloa Road and Kaumaualii Highway, extends not only a warm welcome but a glass of fresh pineapple juice to every visitor. The shipping of pineapples to the Mainland is a specialty, but there's more—just about anything Hawaiian is on sale, and with a smile.

8

Hawaii to Note

ACCESS

United Airlines and Hawaii

Looking back over not inconsiderable travels to and through all the continents, and many of the detached islands of the planet, I can't come up with an airline that has a closer or more successful association with a destination than has United Airlines with Hawaii. Not, heaven knows, that it hasn't paid off for the United. With eight airlines connecting State No. 50 and the Mainland, United captures something like a full juicy third of that traffic.

But there is good reason, and it redounds to the traveler's benefit, and not only because United serves more Mainland cities than any other airline flying to the Islands. United is, after all, nothing less than America's oldest airline, with more than its share of pioneering firsts over the years—first to operate scheduled flights coast-to-coast (1927), first to develop a practical system of two-way plane-to-ground voice radio communication (1929), first transcontinental airline to equip its fleet with radar (1957), first to staff cabins with stewardess crews (1930); first to open a kitchen specifically for inflight food preparation (1936), and—to get to the heart of the subject at hand—first to begin nonstop operations between Hawaii and both Chicago and New York

(1969). United today has 50,000 employees, and flies some 30 million passengers every year. Its routes embrace something like 18,000 miles linking more than 115 cities, with territory ranging from New England and the Atlantic Seaboard through the Southeast, into the Great Lakes, Midwest and Mountain states, and beyond to the Pacific northwest, the Pacific coast from Vancouver south to Mexico, and last, but hardly least, Hawaii.

United's Hawaiian partnership extends over some three decades and coincides with the emergence of Hawaii as both major world tourist destination and the business-commercial hub of the mid-Pacific. The carrier's initial Hawaiian flights were in 1947, via two-propeller DC-6s which constituted the first direct, one-carrier service to Hawaii. These flights helped write the first chapter in Hawaii's post-World War II emergence as a visitor destination of consequence. Pre-Pearl Harbor, Hawaii had been visited principally by affluent holidaymakers with virtually unlimited time (they would mostly go by steamer and stay the winter) and likewise unlimited pocketbooks.

United's first schedules called for daily round-trip hops between San Francisco and Honolulu. In 1947, the grand total on the run was under 17,000. A momentous quarter-century later, in the midseventies, the figure was averaging more than 1.2 million passengers per year between the Mainland and the Islands on regularly scheduled flights, with tens of thousands of additional passengers on United charters.

Those early DC-6 flights were hardly Lindbergh-like as regards austerity. Still the 2,400-mile route from San Francisco to Honolulu took about nine hours westbound and eight hours eastbound at speeds of about 300 miles per hour. Contemporary flight time has been reduced to five hours, by means of United's roomy $23-million, 319-passenger B-747 Friend Ships, which now connect Honolulu with Los Angeles as well as San Francisco, on the West Coast. United planes continue to make nonstop flights between the nation's top two cities—New York and Chicago—with the Islands (The New York-Honolulu run—4,979 miles—is the nation's longest domestic air route). And recent years have seen

United serve a second Hawaiian city, Hilo, on the Big Island of Hawaii, with direct flights from the West Coast.

No United States flag carrier, in my experience, shows more concern, more finesse, nor indeed, more skill in the area of in-flight service. Chances are good that you are not going to be fed a better dinner on a Mainland flight than you will be on United. And in the case of its Hawaiian flights, United goes all out to make each and every one a festive Hawaiian adventure. Invariably, at least one key member of the cabin crew is an honest-to-goodness Hawaiian. All members of the crew are in Hawaiian garb. The girls wear gay, floral-print, ankle-length muumuus, while the men are clad in aloha shirts and white trousers. Meals have delightful Hawaiian touches. And trust United to carry the Island's theme even to such details as the inflight stationery, envelopes and post cards, menu cards, cocktail napkins—all printed in smart Hawaiian designs. You'll even hear piped Hawaiian music in the background.

Other U.S.-Flag Airlines Serving Hawaii

These include *American, Braniff, Continental, Northwest, Pan Am, TWA* and *Western.*

Foreign Airlines Serving Hawaii

Other carriers include Hawaii on routes linking Mainland U.S. cities with South Pacific and Asian points. They include *Air New Zealand, Air Siam, British Airways, China Airlines, Japan Air Lines, Korean Airlines, Philippine Airlines,* and *Qantas Airways.*

By Sea to Hawaii

Time was, pre-World War II, when that was the way to go. You packed an immense wardrobe trunk, took the train to San Francisco, and boarded a Matson steamer, only to alight to the strains of ukuleles and Island songs at the Aloha Tower in downtown

Honolulu. Well, air travel has pretty much replaced the more leisurely ship method. But not entirely. *Pacific Far East Line* bought the luxurious *Monterey* and *Mariposa* from Matson. They connect San Francisco and Los Angeles with Hawaii on cruises that generally schedule stops not only at Honolulu but also at such Neighbor Islands ports as Hilo on the Big Island and Lahaina in Maui. These may be taken in part, and in air-sea combination as well. Additionally, from time to time other major shipping companies such as *Royal Viking* and *Holland America,* to name but two, call at Hawaii in connection with *Pacific and Round the World Cruises.* Travel agents have details. There is some service, as well, on passenger-carrying freighters.

GETTING ABOUT IN HAWAII

Taxis

Taxis are everywhere available, and metered. Your hotel will call one for you. Drivers are generally tipped 10–15 per cent.

Public Buses

Public buses are more an Oahu than a Neighbor Islands mode of transport. (Although in Hilo on the Big Island, there is a small fleet of jitney-type public buses—boldly colored old cars that follow somewhat irregular daytime routes and that are ideal for local color.) The strikingly painted Oahu buses contain but two key words on their sides: *The Bus.*

Persons over 65 may ride for free, but only after obtaining a special pass.

There are two routes of interest to visitors, especially those quartered in Waikiki. They are ⚹2 which goes *ewa,* down Kalakaua Avenue (starting at Kapiolani Park near the Diamond Head border of Waikiki) for such destinations as the Bishop Museum, Mission Houses Museum, Pearl Harbor, Honolulu Academy of

Arts, and downtown, including Iolani Palace, the State Capitol and other attractions of the Civic Center; and ⌗8—for the Ala Moana Shopping Center, Kewalo Basin (Fisherman's Wharf, from which boat tours depart) and the Airport.

For bus route information, ask at your hotel desk or telephone The Bus, 531-5321.

Note also, that Trade Wind Tours operates a shuttle bus service between the two Hilton hotels—the Hilton Hawaiian Village, near the *ewa* frontier of Waikiki, and the Kahala Hilton, a good five miles distant, way around Diamond Head in the Kahala area. The buses run hourly on the hour, between nine in the morning and seven in the evening, stopping at the International Market Place in mid-Waikiki, going in the Kahala Hilton direction. Returning from the Kahala to the Village, departures are on the half hour. There is a charge, but it's much cheaper than a taxi.

The Rent-a-Car Scene

There is a wide choice, including *Avis, Hertz, Budget,* and *National,* among others.

Inter-Island Transportation

By Air: Chances are you will fly. There are two principal airlines linking Oahu with the Neighbor Islands—The Big Island of Hawaii, Kauai, Lanai, Maui and Molokai, with frequent daily departures, especially to the Big Four; fewer to little-visited Molokai and Lanai. These airlines are *Hawaiian Air* and *Aloha Airlines.* Both fly modern jets (Hawaiian's fleet are Boeing 737s, Aloha has Douglas DC-9s) with cabin crews in attendance. Flights are short (most are under a half hour) so that only coffee or pineapple juice are served; no solid food, not even a peanut, let alone a macadamia nut! On most flights, though, alcoholic drinks are available—at a price. During busy times of year, expect crowded air terminals on all the islands, and overtaxed, sometimes minimal staffs, at the Neighbor Islands airports. Inter-island flights are not always fun, but have the great virtue of being quick.

Note that both Hawaiian Air and Aloha flights can be undertaken with what is known as the *Hawaii Common Fare* plan, under which one may fly between Honolulu and Neighbor Islands points for under $10 per hop (this amount is, of course, subject to change) if—note the if—one has a regular round-trip ticket between the Mainland and Hawaii on one of the major scheduled carriers. Certain types of group-fare tickets qualify for the Hawaii Common Fare, too.

Note also, that there is still another inter-island airline. It's called *Royal Hawaiian Air Service;* it flies small craft—Cessna twin-engine 402s—and it is *not* a part of the Hawaii Common Fare arrangement. Take any of its flights and you pay for them, even if you possess a Mainland-Hawaii round-trip ticket. The advantage of Royal Hawaiian is that it flies to some places that Hawaiian Air and Aloha do not, including Kaanapali Beach and Hana on Maui, Upolu on the northern tip of the Big Island and the Kona Village resort on that same island, and Kalaupapa on Molokai. Royal Hawaiian has its own little terminal at sprawling Honolulu International Airport; specify it to taxi drivers.

By Sea: Pacific Sea Transportation operates *Sea Flite*—sleek, speedy hydrofoils on a regular inter-island schedule. Though rapid, they are still slower than planes, although their terminals are usually closer to main hotel areas than the airports. The Honolulu departure point is Pier 8, near the Aloha Tower, downtown. The boats accommodate 190 passengers, are air-conditioned, and with beverage and snack service.

TOURING HAWAII

How to see Hawaii? Make up your mind before you leave home as to whether you want to take an all-inclusive tour—one that includes air fare, hotels, many meals, and some sightseeing. Or whether you want to book only your air fare and hotels in advance, taking care of sightseeing on the spot.

The comprehensive tour is popular with many travelers who have a wide choice of tour packages, including a number of such firms whose specialty is Hawaii, as well as the airlines serving Hawaii.

Examples? Take *Trade Wind Tours,* a giant in the Hawaii field. In co-operation with *United Airlines,* they offer a range of packages—six nights or seven nights in Waikiki with a choice of three categories of hotels and some sightseeing; seven nights divided between Waikiki and the islands of Kauai or Maui; or fortnights embracing Oahu, Kauai, Maui and Hawaii, or simply Oahu, Maui and Hawaii. Additionally, Trade Winds offers other plans whereby stops are made at popular en-route West Coast points such as San Francisco and Las Vegas, usually within a two-week period, with optional visits, for those with more available time, to such destinations as the Grand Canyon in Arizona, and Los Angeles.

Still other packagers who make Hawaii a specialty include *Aloha Hawaii, Hawaiian Holidays, Island Holidays,* and *Mackenzie.* International packagers with Hawaiian tours include *American Express, Cartan,* and *LeBeau.* Your retail travel agent —and you do well, here to choose your agent with care, making sure he is affiliated with the American Society of Travel Agents (ASTA)—can buy the packages of any of these wholesalers for you and fill you in on details on this very moment's tour scene, with this very moment's prices.

But you've arrived in Hawaii with no sightseeing program preplanned. Not to worry. There are a number of organizations on the scene with a variety of day-or-less tours. *Trade Wind,* for example, offers seven daytime excursions—a circle-Oahu journey, another around Honolulu and the Punchbowl, a third to Pearl Harbor (highly recommended, this), and others with destinations ranging from Sea Life Park to a pineapple cannery. After-dark, there are tours taking in night clubs, *luaus,* various spectacles at the hotels, the show at the out-of-town Polynesian Cultural Center, and dinner sails. Other agencies, including *Gray Line, Ha-*

waiian Discovery and *Charley's Scenic,* have similar excursions. There are others that specialize in *custom-made touring*—taking you where *you* want to go, using Cadillac limousines operated by driver-guides. These include *B & G Sightseeing* and *Rainbow Vacation Specialists.*

Still other tours embrace the Neighbor Islands. *Hawaiian Air,* for example, has one-day excursions to Hawaii Volcanoes National Park on the Big Island and Fern Grotto on Kauai; or to Mount Haleakala on Maui; or to Waimea Canyon on Kauai. That same airline has overnighters that go to Kona on the Big Island, Maui, or Kauai. And *Aloha Airlines,* which like Hawaiian Air would be out of business if we didn't want to visit the Neighbor Islands, has similarly attractive propositions. Now, then, if you want to be the first on your block to visit three Neighbor Islands in a hardly relaxing twelve-hour day, there are a pair of companies that can help you out. *Hawaiian Air Tour Service's* itinerary includes put-downs at Kailua-Kona on the Big Island (for lunch) and Kauai (where you visit the Fern Grotto). *Panorama Air Tours* also takes you to Kailua-Kona on the Big Island, the Kahului-Wailuku section of Maui, and then to Kauai, for a Fern Grotto visit, before the return to Honolulu.

There remains, at least on Oahu, *The Bus*—the public bus system, that is, traversing not only Honolulu but much of Oahu. Call Bus Information (531-5321) for tips on the routes and transfers involved in a circle-Oahu journey; it can be fun, and it's cheap.

CLIMATE

The winter daytime average is in the high seventies; in summer, up that to the mid-eighties, with nights as much as twelve degrees cooler than days, year-round. The range in temperature in Honolulu averages only seven degrees between the warmest months (August and September) and the coolest (January and February). Not that it can't exceed the average. Honolulu can go up into the low nineties and down into the mid-fifties.

The water is always nice for swimming—between 75° and 82°. There can be humidity, but in Waikiki it averages 55 per cent, lower than many summer days in Mainland cities like New York, Boston, St. Louis or Atlanta. Northeast trade winds are a kind of natural air conditioner, but there can be times when it becomes uncomfortable, and when people's dispositions are affected; those are the times of the so-called "Kona wind"—coming from the south, and with high humidity as an unwelcome cargo.

As for rainfall, it can go as high as more than 480 inches annually, at Mount Waialeale, in the center of Kauai, but the average for the state is about 70 inches, with Honolulu getting less than half of that. There can be short showers with no notice; normally they are brief and often end with the sun shining and a rainbow resulting. May and June average out as the two months with the least rain, November and December as the months with the most.

On the Neighbor Islands, contrasts can be startling. Mount Haleakala, on Maui, is never sweltering, and it has gone as low as 14°, considerably below the norm. The Big Island's Mauna Kea and Mauna Loa get snow annually in January and February. As for seasons, there are, officially, two: winter extends from October through April; summer, from May through September. My advice: Don't let the weather stop you from going at *any* time of year. Hawaii's climate is one of its greatest assets.

PACKING: LIGHTLY, PLEASE

You say you will, but in the long run, you probably won't. By the time you arrive at your hotel, you have—if you are Mr. or Ms. Average Traveler—given into yourself and taken along too damned much. In Hawaii, of all places, this is bad news indeed. There are two reasons why. First, along with Acapulco and the neighboring Pacific Coast resorts of Mexico, our State No. 50 has become in recent seasons the most delightfully casual-informal major resort in the world; there is no need for really dressy clothes on the part of either men or women. And second: I have never yet met a solitary human being—male as well as female—who has not replenished his wardrobe with Hawaiian-made duds after arrival. (Surely the Hawaiian garment industry is its secret economic weapon.) As with the packing, you make promises to yourself. None of those silly aloha clothes for this kid. What will I do with them at home? Ho, ho. You will wear them at home, and on the next cruise, and the vacation after that on the Côte d'Azur, or wherever. Hawaiian clothes are smart and stylish. Or at least can be, if you know how and where to pick 'em. But that is a matter dealt with in Chapter 7. Here, I only caution you to cut down on quantities of things like shirts (for the men) and just about everything except save undergarments and swimsuits (for the women).

That understood, here are some specific suggestions.

A Basic Woman's Wardrobe

A basic woman's wardrobe—and here I am indebted to Dorothy Chin of the Hawaii Visitors Bureau—should include as much synthetic-fabric clothing as you can manage. Remembering that you will no doubt be purchasing locally, pack one or two pants suits, a pair or two of shorts and slacks and halters, one or two solid-color sweaters for evening and for the mountains, one or two summery long dresses, and possibly a street-length dress or two. If the aforementioned sweaters will not also serve as evening wraps, consider a shawl or stole, or if your visit will be a winter one, a little fur. By no means forget something suitable—and simple enough so that it not clash with whatever you might be wearing—to cover your hair against evening (and sometimes daytime) breezes. Take two bathing suits, each in its own plastic bag so that they can be packed while wet. And wraps for over the bathing suits, as well as clogs or sandals, to be worn to the beach, and otherwise informally. White shoes—a pair or two, and whatever other footwear is required for your wardrobe, remembering that this stuff weighs, and is a bother to pack and repack when going from island to island. Cosmetics by all means, but be assured that they may be replenished with no difficulty on the spot, and may even cost less than at home; Hawaii's sales tax—4 per cent—is cheaper than that in a lot of Mainland areas.

A Basic Man's Wardrobe

A basic man's wardrobe, based upon my own experience, need include only a solitary summerweight suit or navy blazer or sport jacket, and accompanying slacks. I repeat: only a single suit or sport jacket. There are but a handful of places in all Oahu that ask for a jacket at dinner, and even at these, a necktie is optional. The rest of the time, all over Oahu, and absolutely everywhere on the Neighbor Islands, neither jackets nor neckties are worn. Honestly. What you *can* use are several pairs of solid-color slacks. (Checked and plaid slacks, only good with solid-color shirts and jackets, are less practical than solid-color ones—which are the only kind to be worn with the bold-pattern aloha shirts.) I recommend two pairs of white slacks; they're the ones you'll no doubt wear the most. A pair or two of walking shorts if you wear them, and perhaps a pair of blue jeans and/or similarly casual tan slacks. As for sport shirts, pack a few long-sleeved ones, and a few short-sleeved ones. If you have a summer-weight safari or golf jacket, you might take it along. But I assure you, you will buy some aloha shirts—long-sleeved, short-sleeved and short-sleeve modified safari-type (very practical, these) on the spot. Take two swimsuits, each in its own plastic bag, so that they may be packed when wet, a few sets of underwear, a single pair of wash-and-wear pajamas (wash them in the morning, they're dry long before bedtime); several pair of shoes, including a pair of white shoes (loafers are the most versatile), and a pair of sandals for the beach, or for wear with your shorts. Socks can be dispensed with except on the dressiest of occasions. And *please, gentlemen, either short, white athletic socks when you're wearing walking shorts, or better yet—no socks at all. But* never *the dark anklets*

you wear with long trousers at home. There can be the occasional
cool evening or cool excursion into the mountains, when a light
sweater might be handy. Have one or two neckties on hand for
the dressiest restaurants. And your shaving kit, the ingredients of
which are easily replenishable.

For Both Men and Women

Both men and women will want sunglasses (two pairs are not
at all a bad idea, particularly if they are prescription lenses), an
extra pair of eyeglasses and a copy of the prescription, some
Band-Aids, a roll of Scotch tape (it has innumerable uses on a
trip), a few paper clips and rubberbands also are handy; several
plastic bags, some Wash 'n' Dris, or similar premoistened dis-
posable washcloths; an extra cheap ball-point pen or two, a
plastic bottle of aspirin, an anti-diarrhea preparation, a pocket
or purse notebook; names, addresses and phone numbers of friends
of friends back home, to look up; your home country or golf
club membership card, if you plan on establishing exchange
privileges with private clubs in Hawaii; a supply of your personal
and/or business cards, and, I suggest in all modesty, this book!
You'll want to have film for your camera, of course, but if you
run out, you can buy more without difficulty. As for soap and
Kleenex, you have not left the good old U.S. of A.; plenty of both,
everywhere.

Luggage

Luggage? The lighter the better. I have experimented with a
number of designs and materials, but for something like a decade
I have had the same Saks Fifth Avenue canvas bag, with a simple
zipper enclosure, and but two side pockets—no gimmicky built-in-
hangars or flaps. To compartmentalize smaller articles of clothing, I use plastic bags—one for shirts, another for underwear,
etcetera. Women may divide, similarly for their apparel.

Although a Hawaii vacation calls for few garments that wrinkle, it is still advisable to unpack bulkier thins as soon as possible after checking in to a hotel. If you have some wrinkles you'd like removed, hang the garments on a bathroom hook or shower rod, turn on the shower full strength, close the bathroom door and window (if any), and let your garments steam for a while (not forgetting to turn off the shower after seven or eight minutes).

A FEW KEY HAWAIIAN WORDS

You are not going to meet a soul in Hawaii, some Japanese tourists excepted, who will not understand your every word of English. Still, some Hawaiian words and phrases have become an interesting part of the language as it is spoken in Hawaii. Here are some key ones that the visitor does well to know.

Aloha: hello, good-by, love, welcome

Ewa: On Oahu: in a westerly direction

Hale: house

Haole: Caucasian

Kamaaina: island resident, old-timer

Kane: man, or as far as most *malihinis* are concerned, men's room; no cracks about the author of this book, please

Kapu: keep out, forbidden

Keiki: child

Lanai: terrace, porch

Lei: necklace, usually of flowers, seeds or nuts

Mahalo: thank you

Makai: going toward the sea, away from the mountain

Malihini: newcomer

Mauka: going inland, from the sea

Nui: large, great

Waikiki or *Diamond Head* (on Oahu): In an easterly direction

Wahini: woman

(As for pronunciation, a general rule is to pronounce every syllable. The vowels are A as in *blah,* E as in *ay,* I as in *sea,* O as in *old,* U as in *moon.*)

LOCAL LITERATURE

This is a three-newspaper state. Three dailies, that is. In Honolulu—and circulated state-wide—there are the *Advertiser* (morning) and the *Star-Bulletin* (afternoon). They use the same printing plant, but each is separately owned, with separate top managements and editorial staffs, sharing only the advertising and production departments. Of the two, the *Advertiser* is the somewhat more politically liberal. Daily perusal of both papers provide one with an additional dimension of Hawaii, and the way its residents live their non-touristic lives. The amusements pages of both papers keep one up to date on the specifics of day-to-date activity. The *Advertiser,* for example, publishes a calendar called "Today's Leisure" which frequently abounds in ideas for the offbeat—a presentation of the play, *Teahouse of the August Moon,* for example at the Church College of Hawaii, or of *Ulysses in Nighttown* at the University of Hawaii, or of an open-to-the-public student carnival at the venerable missionary-founded Punahou School.

The third daily in the state is the *Hilo Tribune-Herald,* published in the metropolis of the Big Island of Hawaii, and circulated island-wide. The *Maui News* is thrice-weekly—every Tuesday, Thursday and Saturday, while that same island's *Maui Sun* is weekly. On Kauai, the *Garden Island* appears every Monday and Wednesday.

Additionally, free-circulation publications are published on all four major islands for the tourist trade. By no means eschew them; they frequently contain a good deal more than advertising, and can be helpful. Books of Hawaiiana abound; bookshop recommendations on the major islands are to be found in Chapter 7. For a note on television stations, see Chapter 5.

A PERSONAL SLANT ON RECOMMENDED READING

A proper bibliography on Hawaii could make a book in itself. But let me recommend a few background books that I have enjoyed; all are in paperback editions.

Anatomy of Hawaii (Frederick Simpich, Jr., Avon Books). A picture of the state, contemporarily, by a long-time resident.

Calabashes and Kings: An Introduction to Hawaii (Stanley D. Porteus, Charles E. Tuttle Co.). Affectionate, informally written.

Hawaii: An Informal History (Gerrit P. Judd, Collier Books). One must allow for the author's obvious pro-missionary bias— and a lot more that follows as a consequence—given his descent from one of the leading missionary families. Withal, readable and comprehensive.

Hawaii's Story by Hawaii's Queen (By Liliuokalani, published by Charles E. Tuttle Co.). The last of the monarchs wrote this remarkable autobiography after she was deposed. It's fascinating, and provides a nice pro-monarchy balance to the Judd history.

Heroes of Hawaii: The Great Kamehameha and Father Damien (Hawaiai Maikai, Honolulu, publisher). Short but graphic sketches of the state's two major historical figures.

Sarah Joiner Lyman of Hawaii: Her Own Story (Margaret Greer Martin, ed.; Lyman House Museum, Hilo, publisher). A revealing diary and some letters home of a doughty early missionary wife, beginning with her 171-day journey by whaler from New Bedford to Hilo in 1831 and ending in 1883.

The Hawaii Almost Nobody Knows (Alex. H. F. Castro and Harold H. Yost, in paper, with no publisher indicated). Some charming sketches of the Hawaii that was, mostly late nineteenth century onward.

With Lord Byron at the Sandwich Islands in 1825 Being Ex-

tracts from the MS Diary of James Macrae, Scottish Botanist (Petroglyph Press, Ltd., Hilo). The book is not a great deal longer than the title, and makes for absorbing reading. Macrae's Lord Byron was a first cousin of the poet, and his successor to the title. The journey—a sad one—was made for the purpose of returning the bodies of Kamehameha II and his queen from London, where they had both died of the measles.

STATE SYMBOLS

If Honolulu's Iolani Palace (Chapter 2) is America's only ex-royal residence, the *state flag* of Hawaii is the only such, of which Britain's Union Jack is a part. Legends abound how the flag came to be designed as it is. They go back to early British visitors. One such, Captain George Vancouver, met Kamehameha the Great in the late eighteenth century and is said to have presented him with a Union Jack, which came to form the basis of the Hawaiian colors; later—as American influence made itself felt in the Islands—in combination with elements of the Stars and Stripes. The Union Jack is in the upper left corner, and the stripes are alternately red, white and blue. Forms of government have changed in Hawaii, but the flag has remained unchanged through the eras of the monarchy, the republic, the U.S. territory, and statehood. It is unique in this respect among the colors of all 50 states, and it is flown frequently—much more so than those of many states —and with considerable pride. . . . The *state bird* is the gray, gooselike nene, nearly extinct for a while but now to be seen at the zoo in Waikiki and Haleakala National Park on Maui (Chapter 2). . . . The *state song* is "Hawaii Ponoi"; its composer was no less a personage than the last reigning king, Kalakaua, the Merry Monarch. . . . Tropical Hawaii not only has a *state flower*, as do its sister states, but one for each of eight of the islands. The state blossom is the hibiscus, to be seen everywhere in its many variations and colors. The major-island flowers are ilima (Oahu) red lehua (Big Island), lokelani (Maui), and mokihana (Kauai).

THE MONARCHS AND THEIR REIGNS: A RECAP

A monarchy totaling eight sovereigns, with five having the same name, can be confusing, especially when some of the group are known on occasion by secondary names. The role of each monarch's place in Hawaiian history is described in Chapter 1. Still, this table might be handy for ready reference:

Names	Dates of Reign
Kamehameha I (The Great)	1795–1819
Kamehameha II (Liholiho)	1819–24
Kamehameha III (Kauikeaouli)	1825–54
Kamehameha IV (Alexander Liholiho)	1854–63
Kamehameha V (Lot)	1863–72
Lunalilo (William Kanaina)	1873–74
Kalakaua (David Kalakaua)	1874–91
Liliuokalani (Lydia Paki)	1891–93

WORSHIP SERVICES

Courtesy pickup service: The Hawaii Council of Churches operates a nominal-charge bus service that picks up worshippers at a number of leading hotels, deposits them at a number of leading churches, and brings them back after services. Hotel desks have details. The most historic churches (see Chapter 2 for descriptions of these and others, as well) are *Kawaiahao* and *St. Andrew's Cathedral;* both have strong associations with the Hawaiian monarchy, and the former with the early missionaries, as well; these are Protestant. Also on the scene since the mid-nineteenth century is *Our Lady of Peace Cathedral* (Roman Catholic). *Temple Emanuel* (Jewish) is at 2550 Pali Highway. Your hotel desk will have complete information on places of worship as do the church pages of every Saturday's editions of the *Honolulu Advertiser* and the *Honolulu Star-Bulletin;* Neighbor Islands newspapers and hotels are similarly helpful with respect to churches on their islands.

THE TIME

You are way, way out in the mid-Pacific. It is, therefore, two hours earlier than the West Coast, unless the Coast is on daylight savings (which Hawaii does not observe), in which case it is three hours earlier. Add an extra hour for each time zone as you go east on the Mainland, and you can see that planning a long-distance phone call requires some advance calculation.

A CALENDAR OF SELECTED ANNUAL EVENTS

Hawaii loves to celebrate. Given the diversity of its cultural heritage, it finds frequent excuses. Here are some annual events; specific dates—and sometimes even months—vary year to year.

January
Narcissus Festival, Honolulu (Chinese)—may not begin until February.
Hula Bowl—a Honolulu football classic.

February
Haleiwa Sea Spree, Haleiwa, Oahu—celebrating Queen Liliuokalani's birthday.

March
Cherry Blossom Festival, Honolulu (Japanese)—can sometimes start in February or April.
Prince Kuhio Day—statewide celebrations of the birthday of Prince Jonah Kuhio Kalanianaole, Hawaii's first Congressional Delegate.

St. Patrick's Day Parade, Kalakaua Avenue, Waikiki—you guess the date.

April
Buddha Day—all islands.
Merry Monarch Festival—Hilo celebrates the reign of King Kalakaua.

May
Lei Day—everyone, but everyone, gets into Hawaiian togs-cum-*leis,* and celebrates.

June
Kamehameha Day—celebrations honoring Kamehameha I, unifier of the islands—statewide.
Fiesta Filipina, Honolulu.

July
Hawaii State Fair, Honolulu—sometimes also in June.
Rodeos, the Big Island, Maui and Kauai—sometimes also in June and/or August.
Hilo Orchid Society Flower Show—sometimes also in late June.

August
Bon Odori (Japanese)—sometimes also during June and/or July.
Hula Festival, Oahu.
International Billfish Tournament, Kona, Big Island—also sometimes in July.

September
Annual Rough Water Swim, Oahu.
Labor Day Fishing Tournament, Maui.
Hawaiiana Festival, Maui.

October
Aloha Week—statewide and action-packed.

November
Annual Orchid Show, Honolulu.
Kona Coffee Festival, Kailua-Kona, Big Island.

December
Festival of Trees, Honolulu.
International Surfing Championship, Makaha, Oahu.

SOME IMPORTANT TELEPHONE NUMBERS

Oahu Bus Information	521-5321
Tourist Information	
(Hawaii Visitors Bureau)	923-1811
To get the police in the	
Honolulu area	944-1212
To get a doctor in the	
Honolulu area	536-6988
To report a fire (Oahu)	955-1212

FURTHER INFORMATION

The Hawaii Visitors Bureau is funded partly by the State of Hawaii, partly by the visitor-accommodations-transportation industries. It is a valuable and reliable source of free information on Hawaii. Its offices are at 2285 Kalakaua Avenue, Honolulu, Hawaii 96815; 609 Fifth Avenue, New York, New York 10017; 400 North Michigan Avenue, Chicago, Illinois 60611; 209 Post Street, San Francisco, California 94108; and 3440 Wilshire Boulevard, Los Angeles, California 90010. On the spot, in Waikiki, stop into its Visitor Information Office in the Royal Hawaiian Hotel block on Kalakaua Avenue for answers to your questions and brochures on just about any aspect of Hawaiian tourism that is puzzling you. H.V.B. has Neighbor Islands information centers, too: Big Island of Hawaii (Marlin Plaza, Kona, and

180 Kinoole Street, Hilo); Maui (County Building, Wailuku), and Kauai (Lihue Shopping Center, Lihue). *Good maps* of Waikiki, Oahu and the Neighbor Islands are available from the Hawaii Visitors Bureau, at no charge. Additionally, and worth your knowing about: United Airlines publishes a handy little fold-out pocket map of Waikiki, Honolulu and Oahu, while Hawaiian Air publishes a pocket map of Waikiki, with major hotels, restaurants and points of interest indicated; both of these airlines' maps are free and obtainable at their offices.

Acknowledgements

Many friends and colleagues have been helpful in connection with research for the preparation of this book; some are old friends with whom I have worked over the years on assignments in Hawaii. I want especially to thank—alphabetically—for their kindness and co-operation: Kay Ahearn, Marguerite Allen, Jeri Bostwick, Lis Brewer, Simon Cardew, Dorothy Chin, Jacques Cossé, Sheila Donnelly, Max Drechsler, Annette Ebinger, Art Farinas, Ami Gay, Grace Guslander, Mitzi Johnston, Paul and Corazon Kendall, Jim Kennedy, Jim Knaefler, Bobbye Hughes McDermott, Bob Morgan, Loki O'Riley, Jerry Panzo, Harold Rapoza, Roger Ritchie, Hella Rothwell, Sylvia Scott, Maile Semitekol, Phil Shea, John Squire, Sue Sunderland, Alan Wayne, Eddie Wilson, and John Woodruff. Appreciation, too, to Larry Ashmead, my editor at Doubleday; Cathleen Jordan, his assistant; Marie Haller, who copy edited the manuscript; Ellen Povill, who typed it in its final form; and Rafael Palacios, for the handsome map of Hawaii designed especially for this book. Whatever errors crop up are mine, as are, of course, the opinions expressed.

R.S.K.

Index